SAMURAI
IN 100 OBJECTS

For my darling wife Marlene Sandra Turnbull,
on the happy occasion of our marriage on 17 September 2016.

SAMURAI
IN 100 OBJECTS

Stephen Turnbull

FRONTLINE BOOKS

SAMURAI IN 100 OBJECTS

This edition published in 2016 by Frontline Books,
an imprint of Pen & Sword Books Ltd,
47 Church Street, Barnsley, S. Yorkshire, S70 2AS

ISBN: 978-1-47385-038-5

CIP data records for this title are available from the British Library

For more information on our books, please visit
www.frontline-books.com
email info@frontline-books.com
or write to us at the above address.

Printed and bound in India by Replika Press Pvt. Ltd.

Typeset in 9.5/12 Avenir

Contents

Introduction

This book is a celebration of the samurai of Japan, the members of one the greatest military societies in world history. It tells their story through 100 examples of the material culture they left behind, objects which illustrate better than any written records that the samurai were both cruel and cultured, selfish and self-sacrificing, active and artistic.

Samurai warriors carried weapons that were often works of art in their own right and wielded them in a way that was far from beautiful. Their solid iron helmets were designed to absorb the impact of musket balls yet sported fantastic crests of feathers and golden horns. Massive armies ruthlessly burned down palatial enemy castles while comparing themselves artistically to the fragile falling cherry blossom. The samurai repelled foreign invasions and attempted a few of their own, creating along the way a romantic image that the modern age has done nothing to diminish and much to enhance.

Samurai culture, as exemplified by the carefully selected objects gathered here from Japanese locations and from museums around the world, provides a visual expression of samurai tradition, the corpus of their knowledge, beliefs, acceptable behaviour and historical precedents. The formation of the samurai tradition took many centuries because with every major shift in Japanese history the samurai re-invented themselves.

Between the eighth and ninth centuries the word samurai, which originally signified little more than a servant, rapidly came to mean someone who provided service of a specifically military nature. The imperial court of the time, realising the failure of an idealistic programme that had regarded all its subjects as soldiers and conscripted the unwilling to fight inefficiently, seized on the opportunity to commission and reward those who would fight both willingly and well. There was an obvious danger in such an arrangement, as was hinted at in 866 when two district magistrates fought a battle over a border dispute. It was a minor incident, but its significance lies in the fact that neither side had any hesitation about using the official government military forces at their disposal for settling a personal quarrel. The distinction between being commissioned to make war on the emperor's behalf with the forces under one's command and maintaining a private samurai army was becoming dangerously blurred. What is remarkable is how long it took from such a realisation to the time when a serious armed conflict broke out between rival samurai factions at the highest level of state. That development happened with the Gempei War of 1180-85 and resulted in a government of the samurai, by the samurai and for the samurai, with the divine emperor reduced to a figurehead and the real decisions being made by the Shogun, the military dictator whom the powerless emperor had supposedly commissioned to rule Japan on his behalf.

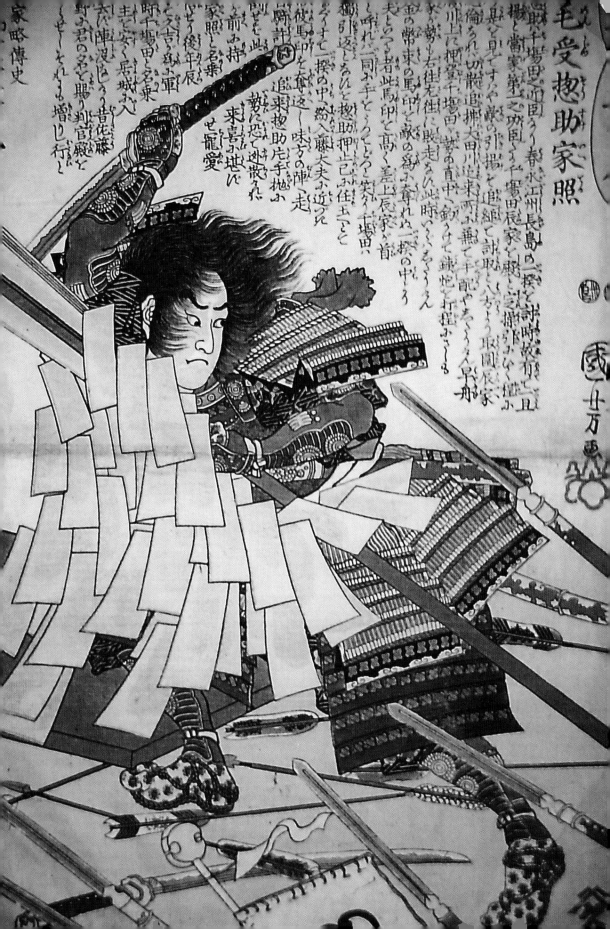

That theoretically temporary commission was not to be handed back to an emperor until 1868. In the meantime the ruling samurai had been the fighting samurai, and those two elements of war and rule went towards creating the artistic, aesthetic, religious, moral and militaristic samurai tradition illustrated here. It was forged during a series of civil wars and culminated in 1600 with the triumph of the Tokugawa family. The Tokugawa Shogunate ushered in a time of peace maintained by force under their iron grip, and just as the samurai who had been killed in battle were enshrined and placated in order to avoid them turning into vengeful spirits, so the whole samurai tradition underwent a profound transformation once there were no battles left to fight.

Samurai culture was harnessed to serve the interests of the ruling class as the samurai became bureaucrats with swords, and then in 1868 the whole concept of the samurai tradition changed yet again. The position of Shogun was abolished and Japan prepared to face the future as a modern nation with one foot stuck firmly in its militaristic past. For the new Meiji government the ideal of a samurai was reinvented and harnessed to inspire Japanese conscript soldiers to die in the name of the emperor. The aristocratic notion of a samurai was quietly dropped. All men were now capable of harnessing the samurai spirit, regardless of their social background.

The subsequent experience of the Second World War produced a further twist, making Japan think again and rejecting any link between its historic military past and its uncertain and tainted recent military present. Instead the samurai were flung back safely into Japan's history to have their stories rewritten, their castles rebuilt and their reputations restored, and in the dusty corners of museums and storerooms the objects shown here were rediscovered. Scraped clean of grime in both a physical and a moral sense, the weapons, armour, scrolls and towers of the samurai tradition could once again tell their true story.

SAMURAI
IN 100 OBJECTS

The Eastern Gate of Fort Akita

秋田城東門

The snow is falling steadily around the bleak Eastern Gate of Fort Akita, an isolated outpost of the imperial Japanese government built in 733 in Tōhoku, the extreme northern part of the main island of Honshū. The fort's walls are made from rammed earth above a shallow foundation of undressed stone. Sandy soil, dug from a depth sufficient to guarantee that no seeds would be present, was mixed with water and carried up ladders to be applied in a series of layers that were firmly rammed down. The final stage was to give the wall a coating of plaster and add a tiled roof to weatherproof it.

The overhanging eaves of the solid wooden gate provide some shelter for the reluctant conscript guards who have been sent to this remote area, although Fort Akita is in fact quite luxurious compared to some of the smaller wooden stockades that it supports out in the forests and mountains. Inside the strong defensive walls is a complex headquarters base from where civilian officials administer these frontier territories. The sentries in the gate house keep a look out for the enemies who are usually referred to as *emishi*, a name that signifies a belief that they are barbarians. They are fiercely independent, and their raids on the forts unsettle the Chinese-inspired civilisation that the central government in Nara is so eager to promote and extend throughout Japan.

A constant supply of troops is needed to defend these precarious outposts, and it may be a request for more soldiers that the official in the smaller picture is writing on one of the wooden strips that were used instead of paper. The men who will be sent north in response to his request will be unwilling conscripts taken from their fields, given a modicum of training and despatched to wild and snowy Tōhoku for years at a time. There is a saying that a man conscripted for military service will be unlikely to return until his hair has grown white, and this largely infantry army are no match for the men who lurk out there in the vast snowy forests of Tōhoku. In fact the system will eventually collapse, and in the year 792 the conscription of farmers will be replaced by something else: the hiring of the highly skilled elite warriors known as **samurai**.

An Ivory Carving of Samurai

武士の象牙の彫刻

In this ivory carving two warriors are shown grappling with each other. They are referred to as *samurai* (literally 'those who serve') and are the followers of powerful local landowners who have been commissioned to fight the emperor's wars in place of the hopeless conscript armies. By the end of the eighth century these trusted warrior families have grown rich in imperial service. Their samurai are highly valued fighters because they are familiar with the areas they live in and have honed their military skills over many decades. Even though the *emishi* problem has been curtailed there are still sporadic dangers from rebels, bandits and pirates, and southern Japan occasionally faces threats of invasion from China and Korea. There is also the need to provide a guard for the imperial capital, a duty that places the samurai at the heart of government.

At first the samurai system worked well, and when rebels arose or succession disputes happened the hired warriors were content to do their duty for the imperial court and receive their just rewards, but it was not long before some serious developments occurred. The ninth century was a time of economic decline marked by plagues and episodes of starvation, all factors that led to resentment against the central government. By the end of the century the embattled court was reluctantly forced to grant far-reaching powers to its provincial governors to levy troops and to act on their own initiatives when disorder threatened.

The first major test for the system happened in 935 with the revolt of Taira Masakado. He was the descendant of an imperial prince who had been sent to the Kantō (the area around modern Tokyo) to quell a rebellion and had been granted the surname of 'Taira', which may be translated as 'the pacifier'. The Taira clan grew to be so important that a minor succession dispute within their family quickly developed into a serious armed uprising against imperial authority. At the height of his rebellion Taira Masakado even proclaimed himself as the new emperor, but an army supplied at a provincial level eventually overcame the revolt and Masakado was beheaded in 940.

Taira Masakado's army consisted of samurai who were elite mounted horsemen supported by foot soldiers. So exclusive did warrior houses like the Taira become that anyone who presumed to wield a bow in the service of the emperor and could not demonstrate that he was of the lineage of a military house stood little chance of promotion or advancement. In 1028, for example, a certain Fujiwara Norimoto who was recognised for his martial accomplishments was sidelined for being 'not of warrior blood'. By contrast, in 1046 Minamoto Yorinobu could reel off a pedigree that went back twenty-one generations. The social elite of the samurai class was now firmly established.

An *ebira* or Quiver

箙

Of all the weapons wielded by the first samurai none was more highly regarded than the *yumi*, the Japanese longbow, for which arrows were stored in an *ebira* (quiver) like the one shown here. It is covered in bear fur and carries a design of a dragonfly. The sharp arrow heads rested securely in the lower basket which would be tied to the samurai's belt, and the feathered arrows, made from the straightest possible bamboo, were withdrawn by lifting them clear of the quiver and pulling them downwards. The wooden reel hanging from the quiver holds a spare bowstring coated with wax to give a hard, smooth surface.

Popular culture may laud the famous samurai sword for being the 'soul of the samurai', but that concept lay a few centuries into the future, and a passage in the chronicle *Konjaku Monogatari* provides a surprise for anyone brought up with the tradition of the sword's priority over the bow. One night some robbers attacked a samurai called Tachibana Norimitsu. He was armed only with a sword, and 'Norimitsu crouched down and looked around, but as he could not see any sign of a bow, but only a great glittering sword, he thought with relief, "It's not a bow at any rate"'.

Norimitsu did in fact vanquish the robbers, but his evident relief that he was not up against anyone armed with a bow is very telling. A bow in the hands of a skilled archer, which is what all elite samurai were trained to be, gave him a considerable advantage over a swordsman who could be incapacitated before he came within striking distance. Nevertheless, the Japanese longbow had nothing like the power of the bows wielded by the mounted warriors from the steppes of Central Asia.

The maximum effective range of a Japanese arrow was unlikely to be more than about 20 metres, and the preferred distance for inflicting a wound or killing an opponent through a weak point in his armour was little more than 10 metres. A further limitation on an archer's skills was that his human target did not usually remain static and was no doubt trying to kill the attacker at the same time. An added complication was provided by the box-like design of the *yoroi* style of armour, which meant that the angle of fire of a bow was considerably restricted. The mounted archer could only shoot to his left side along an arc of about 45 degrees from about 'nine o'clock' to 'eleven o'clock' relative to the forward direction of movement; the horse's neck prevented any closer angle firing.

A Samurai Helmet

兜

The style of armour worn by samurai between the tenth and thirteenth centuries was known as a *yoroi*, and at first sight a *yoroi*, as exemplified by the ornate *kabuto* (helmet) shown here, looks like a very colourful, elaborate and even flimsy version of anything that could be called a suit of armour.

It was put together from several different sections made not from large solid plates or chain mail in the European style but from a number of small scales tied together then lacquered to weatherproof them, a type of armour common throughout much of East Asia. Rows of these scales were combined into strong yet flexible armour plates by binding them together with silk or leather cords. The resulting *yoroi* provided good protection for the body for an overall weight of about 30 kilograms.

The one exception to the lacquered-scale model was the helmet bowl that provided a solid protection for the head, and this modern reconstruction of a typical twelfth century helmet for a high-ranking and wealthy samurai provides an excellent illustration. Helmet bowls were made from separate iron plates fastened together with large projecting conical rivets. A peak, the *mabisashi*, was riveted on to the front and covered with patterned leather, while the neck was protected by a wide and heavy five-piece neck guard called a *shikoro*, which hung from the bowl. The red silk cords that hold the sections of the *shikoro* together would also be found in the body of the armour, giving it a characteristically colourful appearance. The top four plates of the *shikoro* were folded back at the front to form the *fukigayeshi*, which stopped downward sword cuts aimed at the horizontal lacing of the *shikoro*. Normally an *eboshi* (cap) was worn under the helmet as padding, but if the samurai's hair was very long his *motodori* (pigtail) was allowed to pass through the *tehen*, the hole in the centre of the helmet's crown where the plates met. The raised sides of the *tehen* can just be seen. Two lively additions to the basic helmet shown in this example are the grinning *oni* (devil) face on the front of the peak and the slender graceful *kuwagata* (ornamental 'antlers').

Picture Scroll of the Later Three Years' War

後三年の役絵巻

It is difficult not to wince when looking at this contemporary piece of evidence showing the damage a Japanese longbow could do to a human body. The samurai victim, who is displaying immense self-control, has an arrow lodged in his cheek. While one of his comrades holds his head firmly another attempts to extract the broken shaft using a pair of iron pincers. If they are successful he will probably survive.

The samurai's *yoroi* armour on the scroll is much simpler than the one exemplified earlier by the elaborate helmet, because these men are not wealthy generals but ordinary warriors. There are no golden ornaments on their armour, their feet are bare and they sport whiskers, yet all are samurai, as shown by the quivers at their sides, their iron shin guards and the heavy iron helmets.

They are combatants in the 'Later Three Years' War' (*Gosannen no eki*), the curious name given to a fierce war fought between rival samurai clans during the eleventh century. It had its origins in the rivalry between various samurai families who had acquired governorships from the imperial court and then used their positions to enrich themselves. Much political chicanery went into having one's deadliest enemy declared a rebel against the throne. If the ploy was successful anyone who overcame the rebel would expect a reward, and an earlier conflict known as the Former Nine Years' War had made Minamoto Yoshiie (1041-1108) into a hero and a very rich man.

In 1083 Yoshiie set out to vanquish Kiyowara Masahira, a samurai leader who had been his father's ally in the previous campaign. The bulk of the fighting consisted of a prolonged siege of Masahira's stockade fortress of Kanezawa.

Kajiwara Gongorō Kagemasa was sixteen years old, and his descendants would proudly relate that when he received an arrow in his eye at Kanezawa he plucked it out, fitted it to his bow and loosed it at the archer who had delivered the shaft in the first place.

During a lull in the fighting a fellow samurai had attempted to extract the arrow, holding Gongorō down by planting his foot firmly on the wounded man's face. Gongorō would have none of it and vowed that his comrade would pay for the insult with his life.

Such was a samurai's pride, and over a century later one of his descendants would mention this incident in a proclamation of his pedigree before going into battle.

Sword of the *tachi* Style

太刀

No weapon in world history is more closely associated with its users than the Japanese sword and the samurai.

The origins of the deadly curved-bladed sword lay in the straight-bladed swords of Ancient Japan, from which emerged the *tachi*. Early *tachi* and their sword mountings were beautiful objects, as shown on this fine example. The sword illustrated here was actually made in 1827, but it has been forged and mounted in the classic style of a blade that would have been owned by a high-ranking samurai during the twelfth century. The fittings were often works of art in their own right. The wooden scabbard is covered with leather and beautifully lacquered with gilt ornaments. Small, carved metal fittings (*menuki*) lie on top of the *same* (skin of the giant ray) normally bound in tightly by silken cords, traditional decorative features still found to this day. The blade and hilt have gilt copper mounts.

Note the suspensory cords that resemble the cruder models seen on the Gosannen Scroll.

Tachi were slung with the cutting edge downwards from the belts of the early samurai, although it is unfortunate that so few specimens of early *tachi* have survived to provide a useful 'fossil record' of their evolution. One reason for this is that during the Medieval Period many of these fine long blades were deliberately shortened so that they could be worn more conveniently in the later *katana* style with the cutting edge uppermost. As the shortening was done from the tang end such specimens would often lose the signature of their makers, leaving only their provenance or other anecdotal evidence to date them.

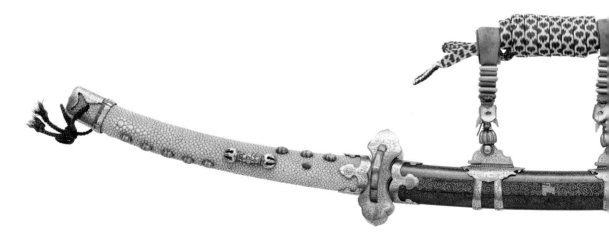

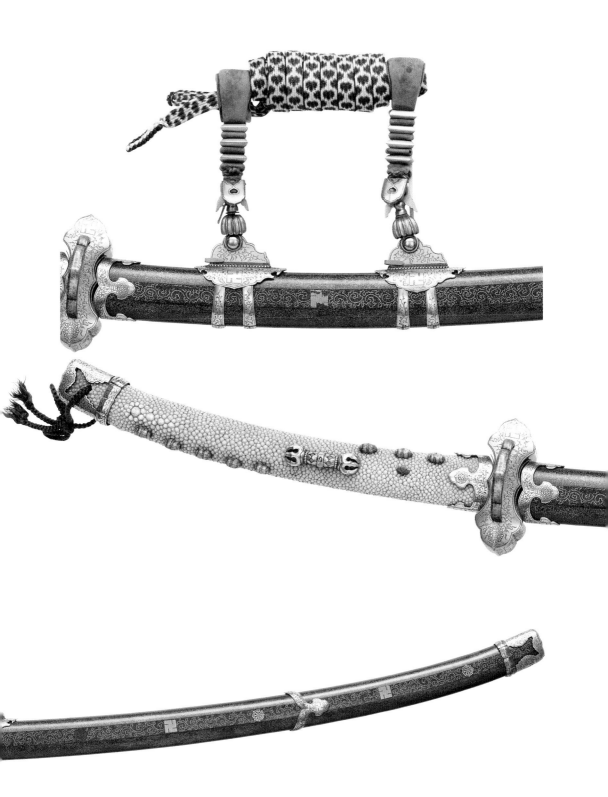

Spiritual Guardian *Niō*

仁王

The face with its tightly clenched mouth is as fierce and expressionless as the stern image that would have been presented by the samurai guards at the gates of the imperial palace. Yet this mute wooden giant is no samurai; he is instead one of a pair of spiritual guardians called **Niō** who protect the entrances to Buddhist temples.

These half-naked giants, illustrated here at a temple on the island of Miyajima in the Inland Sea, are derived from Hindu deities who were incorporated into Buddhist cosmology. One *Niō* would have its mouth open, while the other's mouth was closed, thus symbolising the beginning and end of the universe.

The introduction of Buddhism to Japan happened at the same time as the rise of the samurai and was the beginning of both a religious and a political revolution. Just as the powerful samurai families became integrated into the court's military institutions, so also did Buddhism integrate into its political and religious life to exert an enormous influence on Japan's affairs.

In 794 Japan's capital was moved from Nara to Kyōto via the short-lived Nagaoka. The motive behind the move is usually reckoned to be a desire by the imperial court to free itself from the influence of the great Nara monasteries, and before the new site was selected careful investigations had been undertaken to ensure that the location was suitable according to the Daoist principles of *feng shui. Feng shui* included the belief that evil could attack a city from a north-easterly direction. To the northeast of Kyōto lies a mountain called Mount Hiei, and on top of Mount Hiei there was a Buddhist temple called Enryakuji, which had been founded only six years earlier. It was believed that Enryakuji would protect the new capital against evil, so it was richly endowed and by the eleventh

century the monastery complex consisted of about 3,000 buildings. It was also pre-eminent in the religious education it provided, and there is hardly a name in the annals of eminent Japanese Buddhist teachers and preachers up to the fifteenth century who did not at some time in his life study on Mount Hiei.

For a brief period of time Mount Hiei also became notorious for its *sōhei* (literally 'priest soldiers') who are commonly called warrior monks. These inter-temple or inter-faction disputes were not religious wars as we know them in the West. They did not involve points of doctrine or dogma, just temple politics. In 1113 Enryakuji burned the Kiyomizudera in Kyōto over a rival appointment of an abbot. Enryakuji and its daughter temple Miidera united against Nara again in 1117 in an incident described in *Heike Monogatari*, the great epic of the twelfth-century wars, which quotes the sad words of the ex-emperor Go Shirakawa: 'Three things refuse to obey my will: the waters of the Kamo River, the fall of backgammon dice, and the monks of Enryakuji Temple'.

The traditional weapon of the warrior monks was the long-shafted glaive with a curved blade called a *naginata*. The examples shown in the second illustration are the shaft and scabbard of a variety known as a *nagamaki*, where the blade resembled a sword blade and was almost as long as the shaft itself. Using their *naginata* the monks fought other monks and eventually samurai armies too.

松下加兵衛之綱

川家の謀士秀吉は卜先
綱に仕え初陣えーく
条の先将伊東日向守
討とりいくきろ義元大に
感ぜし之綱ふのとよ
りうて秀吉に
沙駄まし之が
よ秀吉に
じる之綱も
義元のをふひ
恩とせざられべ義
陣没の後へいくくろ
真そ浪人へくと
扶むを浪人へくと
七年秀吉小田原凱陣の
うて晩年大正
うゑこに丹州舟友と
こうて丹州舟友とうるひ

日向守首
藤吉郎討

北条方都水首
養吉郎討

北条方都本
養吉郎討

Head Inspection

首実検

As the wars between samurai rivals continued the traditions of the samurai developed, and one of the most persistent is illustrated here in this woodblock print from the series _Taiheiki Eiyū den_ by Yoshiiku, a pupil of Kuniyoshi.

A sixteenth-century samurai identified as Matsushita Yukitsuna is compiling a list of the severed enemy heads that will be presented before his master Imagawa Yoshimoto (1519-1560). The noble victims have already been identified by tying a name tag to the pigtails. The inscription written on the tag contains the name of the dead man and of the brave samurai who acquired the grisly trophy and thereby demonstrated that he had carried out his lord's wishes. It was no disgrace to lose one's own head in this way, and it could even be regarded as the avoidance of dishonour.

According to custom, the heads of respectable samurai were cleaned and the hair combed before being examined. A major victory would always end with the piling up of dozens, even hundreds, of heads in the commander's quarters for his inspection. _Azuma Kagami_ records that the insurrection of Wada Yoshimori in 1213 yielded 234 heads of defeated warriors.

There is an ironic suggestion included in this print, because Matsushita Yukitsuna's calm appearance shows his blissful ignorance of the fate that would await Imagawa Yoshimoto following a similar head inspection in 1560. Yoshimoto celebrated the capture of one of Oda Nobunaga's frontier castles with the customary head inspection ceremony. He sat in state as the heads were brought before him, but his success had made him careless.

His base within a narrow gorge was only lightly guarded, so Nobunaga took advantage of the situation to launch a surprise attack under the cover of a thunderstorm. Imagawa Yoshimoto at first thought a brawl had broken out among his own troops, but no sooner did he realise what was actually happening than his own head was off his shoulders.

Young Oda Nobunaga (1534-1582) had achieved one of the least expected victories in Japanese history, and very soon it was Imagawa Yoshimoto's own head that became the object of display.

Itsukushima Shrine

厳島神社

Fronted by the sacred deer that roam freely on the island of Miyajima, the huge vermilion *torii* (shrine gateway) of the Itsukushima Shrine appears to float upon the waters of the Inland Sea.

This beautiful religious establishment representative of Shintō ('the Way of the Gods') was the delight of Taira Kiyomori (1118-1181), the most famous head of the dominant Taira family during the early twelfth century. The Taira were physically located around the vital imperial capital of Kyōto and were completely enmeshed in the government of Japan.

As a sea-going clan the Taira had established a formidable reputation for controlling piracy, but their political position had also been helped by a series of dynastic marriages, the suppression of two rebellions and above all by the dominant personality of Kiyomori, who had successfully eliminated all other samurai rivals that sought to emulate his achievements. In 1180 Kiyomori pulled off his greatest political coup when his 2-year-old grandson became the new Emperor Antoku. Not surprisingly, Antoku's succession was challenged, and the subsequent conflict developed into the series of campaigns that are now known as the Gempei War.

Not surprisingly, Taira Kiyomori made many enemies. As a young samurai he had managed to control the militant Buddhist *sōhei* and in a famous encounter with them he had even dared to loose an arrow at the warrior monks' *mikoshi*, the sacred palanquin in which the spirit of the god was believed to dwell. Kiyomori's antipathy to militant Buddhism disguised his own deep

religious commitment, which found chief expression in his endowment of the shrine of Itsukushima. Its position within Taira territory further antagonised the Buddhist establishment around Kyōto and Nara, and satirical stories grew of Kiyomori trying to command the sun to stand still in the heavens so that work could continue on his precious shrine. This is the incident depicted in the accompanying print, a satire on a great statesman and samurai leader.

Minamoto Yoshitsune's Helmet

源義経の兜

This simple iron helmet bowl preserved by the Buddhist temple of Kuramadera near Kyōto is associated with Minamoto Yoshitsune (1159-1189), one of the most famous samurai commanders in the whole of Japanese history.

In spite of being short in stature and of unremarkable physique he inspired his followers to three celebrated victories that brought the Gempei War to a successful conclusion. Legend has embellished much of his life. As a child Yoshitsune was sent away to Kuramadera to become a novice monk, but the military life was more to his liking. He is said to have been taught sword fighting by the *tengu* (goblins) of the forests of Mount Kurama, and his helmet is preserved in Kuramadera to this day. Its authenticity as Yoshitsune's helmet is by no means unlikely, because it was the custom for warriors to donate weapons and armour to shrines and temples with which they had been associated. The helmet is also exactly right for the period, being of heavy iron plates riveted together with an open *tehen*.

Among other legends associated with him Yoshitsune is famous for having defeated the giant monk Benkei, who then became his faithful follower. Minamoto Yoshitsune's reputation as a samurai commander,

however, is much more soundly based and well deserved. At the battle of Uji in 1184 he led a gallant attack across a river to defeat his rebellious cousin Kiso Yoshinaka. The battle of Ichinotani in 1184 saw a similarly daring surprise attack over the edge of a steep cliff, and in 1185 he completed the ruin of the Taira at the battles of Yashima and Dannoura.

Anecdotes about him abound. At the battle of Yashima he risked his life to rescue the bow he had dropped into the water. The reason he gave was that as he was a little man his bow was also small and he did not want to be ridiculed by the enemy because of his size. He was also very brave, and remonstrated with Kajiwara Kagetoki when the latter suggested placing oars in the bows of his boats as well as the stern. That would make them more manoeuvrable when a withdrawal was necessary. Yoshitsune would have nothing to do with retreating, tactical or not, and turned down the suggestion.

Tomoe Gozen

巴御前

Female samurai warriors were a rare yet authentic phenomenon to be found on several historic battlefields, and the most famous one of all is shown on this painting. When Minamoto Yoshitsune gained his important victory over his cousin Kiso Yoshinaka at the battle of Awazu in 1184 Yoshinaka is said to have had at his side his wife Tomoe Gozen. In this painting she is shown fully armoured and wielding a *naginata,* an image derived from the description of her in *Heike Monogatari*, where we read that the beautiful Tomoe Gozen had long black hair and a fair complexion. She was a fearless rider, whom neither the fiercest horse nor the roughest ground could dismay, and so dextrously did she handle sword and bow so that (in a phrase much used to describe any samurai, male or female) she was 'a match for a thousand warriors, and fit to meet either god or devil'.

The battle of Awazu was to be her last fight, and when all the other samurai had been slain or fled, among the last seven loyal followers of Yoshinaka rode Tomoe Gozen. Yoshinaka would be killed by an archer when his horse became mired in a frozen paddy field. After describing Yoshinaka's final manoeuvres the *Heike Monogatari* account returns to Tomoe Gozen as follows:

'But now they were reduced to but five survivors, and among these Tomoe still held her place. Calling her to him Kiso said, "As you are a woman, it were better that you now make your escape. I have made up my mind to die, either by the hand of the enemy or by mine own, and how would Yoshinaka be shamed if in his last fight he died with a woman?" Even at these strong words, however, Tomoe would not forsake him, but still feeling full of fight she replies, "Ah, for some bold warrior to match with, that Kiso might see how fine a death I can die!" And she drew aside her horse and waited. Presently Onda no Hachirō Moroshige of Musashi, a strong and valiant samurai, came riding up with thirty

followers, and Tomoe, immediately dashing into them, flung herself upon Onda and grappling with him, dragged him from his horse, pressed him calmly against the pommel of her saddle and cut off his head. Then stripping off her armour she fled away to the Eastern Provinces.'

That is the last we hear of her in *Heike Monogatari*, although other romantic sources add that Yoshinaka expressly directed her to take the story of his final battle back to their home province of Shinano. Before leaving the field she was attacked by Wada Yoshimori using a pine trunk as a club. She twisted the trunk in her hands and broke it into splinters, but Wada Yoshimori caught her and made her his concubine. She was to bear him a son, the celebrated strong man Asahina Saburō Yoshihide who was killed in 1213 when the Wada family were destroyed by the Hōjō. Tomoe then became a nun and lived to the age of ninety-one. With that Japan's greatest female samurai warrior would pass out of history.

23

A Heike Crab

平家蟹

Look closely at the shape of the shell of this crab and you may discern the face of the dead samurai whose spirit, according to legend, dwells within. If so, that samurai from the Taira family (the Heike) was one of thousands to perish during the battle of Dannoura, the sea battle whereby the Gempei War came to an end in 1185.

Dannoura was one of the most decisive and remarkable conflicts in Japanese history. Its decisiveness lay in the utter destruction inflicted upon the Taira, while its remarkable nature lay in the final and complete reversal of the balance of superiority between land and sea warfare enjoyed by the two rivals. At the battle of Yashima scarcely a month earlier Minamoto Yoshitsune had tried to avoid a naval action at all costs; now he chose to engage the Taira on what appeared to be a watery battlefield of their own choosing.

Confident in their seagoing ability the Taira had sailed up the Straits of Shimonoseki, eager to inflict a quick victory on the Minamoto fleet before the tide turned against them. But traitors in their midst revealed to the Minamoto on which ship the Taira has concealed the child emperor Antoku. The fight was then concentrated on this target, so the boy's grandmother jumped into the sea with him to avoid his capture. With the emperor dead and the battle lost the Taira leaders too drowned themselves. The final suicide was that of their leader Taira Tomomori (the son of the great Kiyomori), who put on two suits of armour to weigh his body down and also held on to an anchor, as shown in the accompanying picture. *Heike Monogatari* then provides the visual image that was to become the enduring memory of Dannoura. 'Now the whole sea was red with the banners and insignia that they tore off and cut away … while the white breakers that rolled up on the beach were dyed a scarlet colour.' Some made it back to the Taira base on the island of Hikojima,

and these survivors were to provide the later legends of 'Heike villages', isolated hamlets in the mountains where survivors of the Taira lived anonymously for generations.

Beside the beach of Dannoura the massacre was almost total, and the other powerful legend associated with Dannoura are these so-called Heike crabs who live in the vicinity. Ghost stories also developed that told of dead warriors rising from the waves to attack any ships containing the Minamoto who passed through the Straits of Shimonoseki, a theme that found expression in the Noh theatre. Nowadays the graves of the Taira lords who perished at Dannoura are located at the rear of the Akamagū, the shrine on the shore that was raised to comfort the spirit of Emperor Antoku. This place provides the focus for commemoration of the great battle with which the Gempei War came to a tremendous end as thousands of samurai perished to live on as ghosts within the Heike crabs.

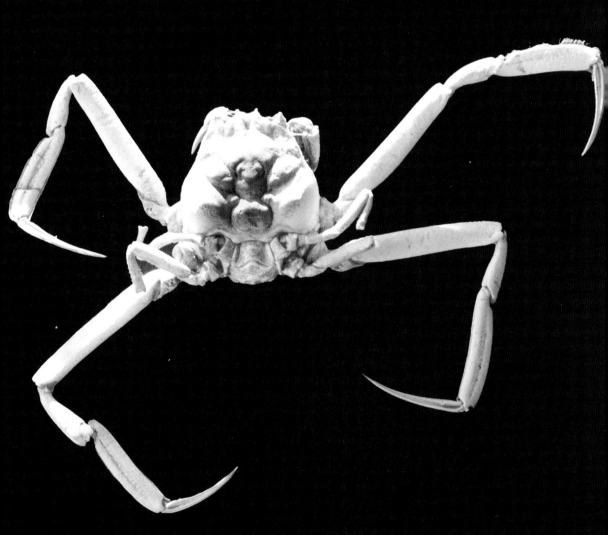

A Mongol Bomb

震天雷

In 1274 the samurai were introduced to the destructive effects of gunpowder for the first time, and this iron-cased bomb excavated from a wrecked Chinese ship was the means by which the innovation was delivered.

Ceramic bombs and simpler solid stone projectiles were also found on the ships that were sent against Japan during invasion attempts by the Yuan (Mongol) dynasty of China. Their repulse by the samurai is celebrated as one of the most glorious episodes in Japanese history. The first attack provided several surprises for the Japanese defenders who had been used to a mode of combat that valued individual challenges and archery duels. Instead they were faced with phalanxes of infantry archers who loosed anonymous clouds of arrows against the waiting horsemen, but the biggest shock of all came from the launching of the exploding bombs.

Called in Chinese *zhen tian lei* ('the thunder which shakes the heavens') they were spheres of iron or ceramic material filled with gunpowder and shrapnel and ignited by a time fuse. The bombs were thrown from simple lever catapults operated by trained teams of men working in unison. In the smaller illustration we see one of the bombs exploding. The picture is based on a contemporary document that one of the samurai generals had painted to back up his claim for reward.

For many centuries no one knew for certain what the exploding bombs looked like, but at the end of the twentieth century samples were found among the remains of some wrecked Mongol ships off the island of Takashima. They had been destroyed by the ferocious typhoon that battered the fleet as it lay at anchor ready for a second invasion attempt in 1281. The storm was immediately regarded as the work of the gods and delivered in answer to prayer, so it was dubbed the *kamikaze*, the wind from the gods.

The same word was to be applied to the suicide pilots who tried to defend Japan in 1945.

The 'Chrysanthemum on the Water' Crest

菊水紋

A *noren* (curtain) hangs limply in the wind at the entrance to a temple in Yoshino that is associated with one of Japan's greatest samurai heroes. Its design gives a clue as to who he is, because it is a *mon* (family badge or crest) showing the imperial chrysanthemum floating on the water.

The chrysanthemum motif is used only to symbolise the emperors of Japan, so its incorporation into a samurai's badge indicates that its owner was very special. The warrior was Kusunoki Masashige (1294-1336), the loyal supporter of Emperor Go-Daigo, hence the image of the imperial flower being borne above the waves in safety.

The background to the Kusunoki story is as follows. The victory by the Minamoto over the Taira during the Gempei War had relegated the status of the emperor to that of a ceremonial and religious figurehead under the overall rule of the Shogun. During the early twelfth century the position of Shogun was also temporarily diminished by the Hōjō family who ruled as regents. It was they who had bravely resisted the Mongol invasions, but in the mid-fourteenth century their rule received an unexpected challenge in the person of Emperor Go-Daigo who wished to restore the imperial power to what it had been when emperors sent loyal warriors off to fight on their behalf. Go-Daigo's rebellion attracted the support of a number of samurai families who disliked the Hōjō. Among them were the Ashikaga and the Kusunoki, and between them they brought about the restoration of the imperial

power. Sadly, arguments then began about the rewards that the samurai expected and a further war broke out.

The Ashikaga took the dramatic step of choosing their own emperor who then proclaimed them as the Shogunal family. Japan consequently had two emperors: the 'Northern Court' under the Ashikaga in Kyōto, and the fugitive 'Southern Court' of Go-Daigo in exile in the mountains of Yoshino. The sporadic set of battles that followed became known as the Nanbokuchō Wars (the wars between the southern and northern courts).

Of all the samurai commanders who stayed loyal to Go-Daigo the most celebrated name is that of Kusunoki Masashige. He led a very successful guerrilla campaign in the mountains of Yoshino, but tragedy struck when Go-Daigo ordered him to take on the advancing army of Ashikaga Takauji in a field battle. Masashige knew that the situation was hopeless, but his loyalty to the emperor gave him no option other than to obey. Before leaving for battle Masashige bade farewell to his young son Kusunoki Masatsura, whom he charged with continuing the struggle after his father was dead, the theme of the smaller picture.

Masashige did indeed die at the subsequent battle of Minatogawa in 1333.

At the time of the Meiji Restoration in 1868 Kusunoki Masashige was 'discovered' as the ideal of loyalty to the emperor, and his example was urged upon the supporters of another imperial restoration. His statue now stands outside the Imperial Palace in Tokyo and the shrines and temples where he is honoured remember him by the symbol of the chrysanthemum on the water.

The Temple Door of the Nyoirinji

如意輪寺の扉

One of the doors of the Nyoirinji, a temple in Yoshino that once provided a refuge for the Southern Emperors, bears a poem scratched into its surface using an arrow head. It reads:

I could not return, I presume
So I will keep my name
Among those who are dead with bows'.

The stanzas were carved in 1348 as a farewell death poem by Kusunoki Masatsura (1326-1348), who had been entrusted by his father, Masashige, with the task of continuing the struggle against the Ashikaga on behalf of the rightful emperor. The request had clearly not fallen on deaf ears even though the boy had only been ten years old at the time. He quickly grew to manhood and in 1347 became the leader of the supporters of Go-Daigo's successor against the Ashikaga.

His early victories led Ashikaga Takauji to send a large army against him in 1348, forcing Masatsura to withdraw to Yoshino, where he was gratefully received by the exiled Southern Emperor. Profoundly moved by the reception, Kusunoki Masashige wrote his final poem on the door and then left to met his death at the battle of Shijō-Nawate.

Poems written immediately before death were a highly valued element in samurai tradition and derived from the example first set by Minamoto Yorimasa (1106-1180) at the battle of Uji. Yorimasa wrote a poem on his war fan before committing *seppuku* (suicide by opening the abdomen), a very painful method of dispatch popularly called

hara kiri. That set the standard, but Kusunoki Masatsura's farewell poem was not to be the most dramatic version to follow Yorimasa's lead. One warrior during the sixteenth century is supposed to have written a poem on another temple door using the blood from his own severed abdomen.

Wooden Statue of Ashikaga Takauji

足利高氏木像

In the spring of 1863 a very unusual thing happened in Kyōto. Nine men broke into the temple of Tōji-In. They were all political activists of the samurai class who were loyal to the Emperor and opposed to the continuing rule of the Tokugawa Shoguns.

The raiders cut the heads off their intended victims, one of whom is shown here. Beheadings were not uncommon in Japan during that turbulent time, but these decapitations were very different because the heads came from three wooden statues.

The effigies were of three Shoguns, but they were not from the ruling Tokugawa family to whom the insurgents were so violently opposed. They were instead statues of the first three Shoguns of the Ashikaga dynasty: Takauji (1305-1358), Yoshiakira (1330-1368) and Yoshimitsu (1358-1408). All had lived centuries before the Tokugawa rose to power.

As a clue to their motivation, one of the raiders wrote a long poem when he was in prison following the incident. It included the words, 'Takauji, you and your disgusting son betrayed the emperor and tormented the princes. You are unparalleled traitors to the country'.

What was it about the Ashikaga family that aroused such ire in the samurai of the nineteenth century? The answer lies within the enigma that is known as samurai loyalty. Kusunoki Masashige and Masatsura had responded enthusiastically to Go-Daigo's call to arms.

Their long service and their refusal to change sides led to the Kusunoki becoming the imperial hero family. Ashikaga Takauji's achievements were far greater than Masashige's, but the fact that he first opposed Go-Daigo then supported him, and finally abandoned him, coupled with Takauji's presumption to die 'with his boots off' has made him into the ultimate samurai anti-hero. The split between the two imperial courts was his doing, so Takauji would become Japan's greatest samurai villain. Little more than 100 years ago any visitor to Tōji-In could borrow a wooden paddle and give the Ashikaga shoguns a good walloping!

The Scroll *Boki Ekotoba*

慕帰絵詞

Is the enigmatic figure shown on the left of this scroll a female samurai in full armour? Tomoe Gozen was introduced earlier as one of the few examples of samurai women warriors, and whereas written descriptions are difficult to come by, contemporary illustrations are virtually unknown.

One possibility is the scroll called *Boki Ekotoba*, which was painted in 1351. Written by Jishun (1295-1360) and illustrated by Kakunyo (1270-1351) the scroll, which is owned by the Nishi-Honganji in Kyōto, contains exquisite detailed pictures of contemporary life. In the section shown here a wandering *biwa* (lute) player is shown entertaining three people. It was the practice of such itinerants that they would recite the great epic of the destruction of the Taira family known as *Heike Monogatari*, from which several quotations have been used in this book. Those sad tales of heroism and self-sacrifice added greatly to the samurai tradition as the centuries went by.

The *biwa*'s three listeners are armoured and two have a monk's shaven head, but the figure on the left appears to be female. She is kneeling and wearing full armour. In her right hand she grasps the shaft of a bow, while a *naginata* lies across her lap with its blade protruding from the window.

It is possible that the figure is meant to represent a youth, but her features are very feminine with rouged cheeks and painted eyebrows, and by comparison the faces of all the other characters are coarse and masculine. The most intriguing conclusion is that she was a wife or daughter of one of the *sōhei* who is fully armed ready for battle.

A *wakizashi* Sword

脇差

This is a **wakizashi** forged by Yasutomo of the Mishina School in Osaka and dated 1807. **Wakizashi** is the name given nowadays to a short Japanese sword, reflecting the fact that most contemporary illustrations of samurai in armour show them with two sidearms rather than just one.

Modern students of Japanese arms and armour and connoisseurs of swords now employ the words *tachi*, *katana*, *wakizashi* and *tantō* to identify various types of Japanese edged weapons, but these words have more to do with classifying swords artistically. Commonly, a *wakizashi* is the short sword that together with a *katana* (the sword thrust through the belt with its cutting side upwards rather than being slung from a belt) makes up a *daishō*, a pair of swords furnished with identical designs of mounts and fittings. A *tantō* is a shorter bladed weapon usually translated as 'dagger'.

Historically, it is better to approach the subject from the point of view of what was actually worn at a samurai's side, where would be found one long sword in a slung scabbard in *tachi* style (as illustrated earlier) and at least one other subsidiary edged weapon worn through the belt for purely practical reasons. Using the modern terminology these 'companion side arms' are either *wakizashi* or *tantō*, and it was long believed that *wakizashi* were worn beside a *katana* in civilian dress while the even shorter *tantō* was worn only when armoured.

However an examination of contemporary portraits calls this assumption into question. A famous hanging scroll depicting Honda Tadakatsu (1548-1610) in armour shows him wearing not one but two companion swords that look like the conventional 'wakizashi' and 'tantō'. The *wakizashi* is worn on his left side and the *tantō* on his right. By contrast, a painted scroll of his contemporary Naitō Ienaga (1546-1600), who died at the siege of Fushimi during the Sekigahara campaign, shows him in armour wearing a short-bladed weapon as his companion arm but with a long sword worn *katana* style, Quite clearly there were no hard and fast rules about how many weapons should be worn or how they should be carried.

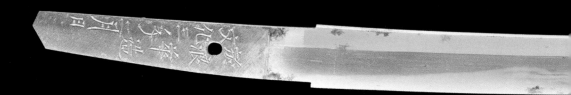

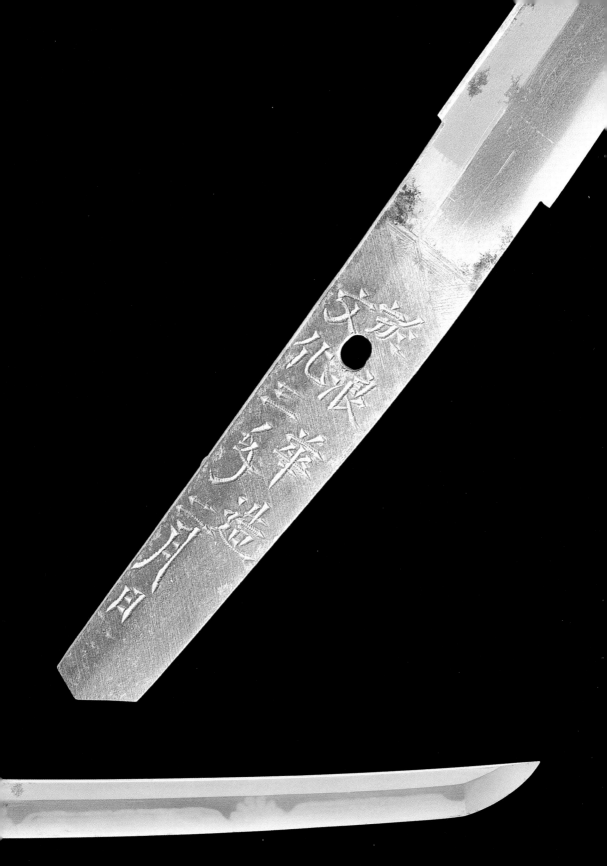

37

The *wakō*

倭寇

In this painting from the National Military Museum in Beijing we see Chinese troops battling against sea raiders who are ravaging the coast. The Chinese defenders have round shields and one is using a forked tree branch to catch the pirates, all of whom are armed with Japanese swords.

The name given to the pirates appears in Chinese as *wokou*, and in Korean it is pronounced *waegu*. In each case the first character in the two-ideograph word is the ancient name given by the inhabitants of China and Korea to Japan, which shows clearly where they believed that their tormentors had come from. In many cases the identification was correct and the name for a pirate entered the Japanese language as *wakō*.

Piracy in the Far East was by no means confined to one country of origin, and by the mid-sixteenth century individual pirate bands had acquired a decidedly multinational character. Chinese, Korean and even Portuguese freebooters were involved in massive raids on coastal communities. Some of the most influential pirate leaders were renegade Chinese who based themselves on the Japanese islands and sailed from there to terrorise their fellow countrymen under the convenient anonymity of *wakō* and with a strong emphasis on the character 'Wa'.

Earlier *wakō* raids, however, can be unmistakably linked to Japan. In 1223 gangs of Japanese pirates launched attacks on Korea's southern coast from locations on the northern coast of Kyushu and the islands of Iki and Tsushima. Further raids followed in 1225, 1226 and 1227, and are well documented in both Japanese and Korean sources. For example, one Korean accounts tells us that in 1225 'two Japanese ships raided the coastal prefectures and sub-prefectures of Kyŏngsang Province. Troops were dispatched and captured them all.'

Portraits of the *wakō* were presented to the Korean ruler so that he could see what they looked like. In 1350 six large *wakō* raids took place on Korea, and for the next 25 years the records show an average of five a year. The peak was reached between 1376 and 1384 when the average rose to over forty a year, but these raids were no mere pirate raids on coastal towns. As many as 3,000 *wakō* are known to have been involved in some operations. Nor did their raids stop at Korea, because it was during the 1350s that piracy against China began in earnest. Small raids had been carried out on the Ningbo area between 1308 and 1311, but in 1358 the Shandong peninsula was raided in a major attack, while other bands struck in Jiangsu and the coastal provinces south of the Yangzi delta.

The Temple of the Golden Pavilion

金閣寺

Kinkakuji, the 'Golden Pavilion', shines in the evening light beside the pond that acts as a mirror. It is a gem of Japanese architecture and will forever be associated with the great Shogun Ashikaga Yoshimitsu (1358-1408).

Yoshimitsu was the renaissance prince of Japan who not only brought an end to the schism between the Southern and Northern Courts but also promoted trade relations with China and patronised art and culture on a grand scale. The present Kinkakuji is a replacement after its destruction by an arsonist in 1950, and its original form contained some remarkable interior features that expressed the syncretic nature of Japanese religion. The ground floor housed a statue of Amida Buddha. The next floor up had a statue of Kannon the Goddess of Mercy, while the uppermost floor was a Zen sanctuary.

Yoshimitsu had become Shogun in 1367. By 1374 the supporters of the Southern Court were in defeat and disarray almost everywhere in Japan, so the Southern Emperor Go-Kameyama was persuaded to submit and transferred the imperial regalia to Go-Komatsu, the Emperor of the North. There would still be sporadic risings in the name of successive heirs to the Southern Court over the next half century, but none lasted long, and Yoshimitsu deserves the credit as the man who brought reconciliation and peace to Japan. He also took a strong line on the matter of the *wakō*. Embassies were set up with China and trade was encouraged, a matter in which Yoshimitsu was very fortunate because the Yuan dynasty had recently been overthrown and replaced by the Ming. The time was right to repair the damage that had been caused to relations by the Mongol invasions.

Ashikaga Yoshimitsu therefore combined almost every role that a Shogun could have: politician, warrior and aesthete in one consummate individual, and the Golden Pavilion is his stunning memorial. With such a list of achievements under his belt it is surprising to hear that Yoshimitsu's wooden effigy was included in the ritual decapitation at Tōji-In described earlier. The testimony read, 'The mad and treacherous Yoshimitsu is a criminal who went begging to the king of China, demeaning himself to become the king's retainer, and polluting the divine country'.

The reference is to Yoshimitsu accepting the customary (and largely meaningless) tributary relationship that China enjoyed with its neighbours, whereby they paid notional tribute to the Chinese Emperor and were supposedly re-invested with their own titles as rulers of their own countries. Yoshimitsu considered that it was a price worth paying to restore harmony. Certain of his rivals disagreed, and as the 1863 incident showed, it was a resentment that lingered for centuries.

Marishiten

摩利支天

The religious beliefs of the samurai class were rich and varied. All samurai were imbued with the traditions of the numerous **kami** who provided the focus of worship in Shintō, while Buddhism provided many other gods, rituals and beliefs. To the Zen Buddhism espoused by Ashikaga Yoshimitsu and many other notable samurai we now add the cult of Marishiten (Mārīcī in India), who has acted in many roles over the centuries in both a female and a male form. Here we see Marishiten as a very male-looking warrior deity with three heads, six arms and riding upon a wild boar. He is wearing Chinese armour. One pair of his hands control a spear, another a bow and arrow, while the remaining two hands hold a sword and a war fan.

Marishiten, therefore, looks like an ideal deity for a samurai to worship, and in fact he offered one extra and unique blessing to a warrior because Marishiten was the god to whom one prayed if one wanted to become invisible. Such a desire and belief may sound surprising, because warrior epics such as *Heike Monogatari* strongly suggest that once on the battlefield the samurai made every effort to be seen. This was especially true in the earlier wars when warriors shouted out challenges to each other before engaging in battle and proclaimed their glorious pedigrees in a world of open combat between honourable opponents. Yet the 'invisibility' sought from Marishiten was not necessarily of a physical nature. It could indicate a range of techniques from hiding one's strategic or tactical intentions to the psychological confusion of an enemy swordsman during hand-to-hand combat. A warrior therefore became 'invisible' if his enemy's mind was confused and his own was clear, and it was to these qualities that a Marishiten devotee aspired.

As a result, Marishiten provided unique help in attaining victory by confusing enemies in various ways. She/he has also been a healer, a protector of travellers and a *bodhisattva*, a saint-like Buddhist figure who has undertaken not to attain enlightenment until all mankind are saved. Kusunoki Masashige was devoted to Marishiten, and had her name written on one of his banners. In practical terms most of the Marishiten-orientated rituals performed by samurai were the utterance of relatively simple prayers, but they also included supposedly magical spells and the use of *mudra* (esoteric hand gestures made by twisting the fingers in various patterns). The latter are quite common in Japanese Buddhism but have received great prominence in popular culture because of their association with ninja.

No textbook on ninjutsu is complete without some reference to the mystical nine hand gestures that the secret warrior would make, either to confuse his enemies or to achieve invisibility. The cult of Marishiten is the simple origin of all these gestures, which were by no means unique to ninjutsu, and the deity remains an important if little-recognised entity in Japanese religion.

Helmet Crest of Fudō Myo-ō

不動明王の前立

Marishiten may have been a popular warrior deity among some samurai, but his cult was by no means as popular as that of Fudō Myo-ō ('the immoveable wisdom king'), shown here in the form of a *maedate* (front crest) on a helmet dating from the late sixteenth century.

The Myo-ō group of deities are wrathful and warlike gods who represent the power of Buddhism to overcome passion. Fudō, the best known of the group, is an emanation of Dainichi Nyorai, one of the five Buddhas of wisdom. He seeks to convert anger into salvation and may even be regarded as frightening believers into accepting Dainichi Nyorai's teachings. He is indeed an intimidating character, as the figure on the helmet brings out. His face is fierce and he sometimes has a third eye. Other versions of him have one tooth sticking upwards and another pointing down, or his teeth are seen biting his lip.

The spear he carries in his right hand represents wisdom cutting through ignorance and is often replaced by a sword with the same message. Usually he will also have in his left hand a rope to catch and bind demons. Here he is seated on a rock, a symbol of his characteristic immovability. Paintings of Fudō usually depict him either in red or in blue. In Shingon temples dedicated to Fudō the priests perform *goma* (burning) rituals to honour him and enlist his power of purification.

Fudō's strength of purpose and ferocity of appearance endeared him to many samurai. The great warlord Takeda Shingen commissioned a portrait to be painted of himself in the likeness of Fudō as a deterrent to his enemies, and a similar motivation may lie behind the choice of Fudō for a helmet badge.

The *mon* (family badge) which appears on the fukigayeshi (*turnbacks*) cannot be identified but consists of three triple *tomoe* (commas) arranged in a triangular pattern. The Fudō figure is nicely arranged in front of three golden lotus leaves. The combination of the immovable god and the fierce expression on the iron face mask presents an image of resolution and intimidation that was the samurai's stock in trade.

45

23

Sword of *katana* Style

刀

Katana is the Japanese word most commonly used to identify the deadly curved-bladed sword of the samurai, the final evolutionary stage of the finest edged weapon in world military history.

As noted earlier, the *tachi* style of sword was slung from the belts of the early samurai. Its transformation to the *katana* had less to do with shape and construction that with its mode of use because a *katana* was thrust through the belt with the cutting edge uppermost. The samurai could then deliver a deadly sword stroke as part of the action of drawing his weapon rather than by means of a two-handed movement of unsheathing and preparation.

Nowadays swords are classified as either *tachi* or katana depending upon which side of the tang contains the maker's signature. The reason for this is that the signature of the maker was traditionally carved on to the side of the tang that was on the outside of the sword when being worn. A *katana* therefore had the signature on the opposite side of the tang from the *tachi*.

The *katana* was the weapon that was to become the samurai sword of legend. When lying in its position of rest, the sword worn through his belt in civilian dress told the world that its owner was indeed a true samurai. He was the member of a social and military elite because the lower classes in Japanese society, theoretically at least, did not carry weapons. When drawn from the scabbard, an event that occurred mercifully less frequently than movies would have us believe, the *katana* became the ultimate means of asserting the samurai's authority.

On the battlefield the *katana* was the supreme edged weapon, but for skills in swordplay, as distinct from simply killing as

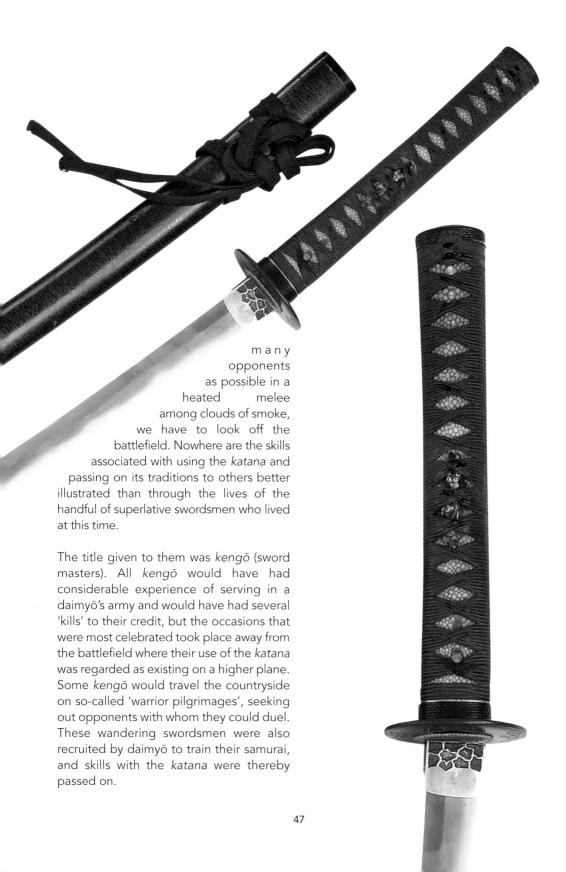

many opponents as possible in a heated melee among clouds of smoke, we have to look off the battlefield. Nowhere are the skills associated with using the *katana* and passing on its traditions to others better illustrated than through the lives of the handful of superlative swordsmen who lived at this time.

The title given to them was *kengō* (sword masters). All *kengō* would have had considerable experience of serving in a daimyō's army and would have had several 'kills' to their credit, but the occasions that were most celebrated took place away from the battlefield where their use of the *katana* was regarded as existing on a higher plane. Some *kengō* would travel the countryside on so-called 'warrior pilgrimages', seeking out opponents with whom they could duel. These wandering swordsmen were also recruited by daimyō to train their samurai, and skills with the *katana* were thereby passed on.

Castle Tower of the Sengoku Period

戦国時代櫓

A sentry mounted at the top of this free-standing *yagura* (tower) of the reconstructed Arato Castle near Ueda in Nagano Prefecture would have a view of the whole of the river valley below. Typical of the time, this *yamashiro* (mountain castle) was the model of Japanese fortress that would see hundreds of examples of attacks by samurai armies on the territories owned by the opportunistic samurai warlords who went under the name of daimyō (literally 'big names'). They owed their existence to a civil war known as the Ōnin War that began in 1467 and ushered a century and a half of conflict that historians compare to the Sengoku (Warring States) Period in China. The techniques and traditions of samurai warfare developed quickly during the Sengoku Period as did the technology of building a Japanese castle, so by the end of the sixteenth century Japanese castles looked very different from the simple Fort Akita discussed earlier. The most common type of fortification was a *yamashiro*, so-called because the earlier varieties were little more than a series of palisades and simple buildings erected around the existing contours of a mountain.

During the Sengoku Period a technique began whereby the mountain itself was modified by sculpting its shape into something more defensible. Slopes were raised, ditches were cut between spurs and artificial gullies were scooped out down which boulders could be rolled. The various natural sections of the mountain were also levelled off, resulting in a rough stockaded structure with tall lookout towers, gates and wooden buildings set upon and among the natural contours of a hill with considerable effort being made to adapt and enhance those contours using man-made ditches, ramparts and levelled terraces. A *yamashiro* was therefore carved as much as it was built, and we also must banish from our minds any image of a Japanese castle based on elegant later specimens with golden decorations, soaring tiled roofs, huge stone bases and plastered walls. Almost no stone was used to augment a *yamashiro*'s

defences, into which rocky cliff faces and high peaks were incorporated instead. Rivers often provided natural moats.

In many cases a daimyō's *yamashiro* was not intended for residential use. It was an earth and timber strongpoint at which an army could gather in times of war and in which the local population could find refuge. It provided a defensible position, gave an excellent viewpoint and defied attack by its strong palisades and steep mounds. Most importantly, all these features could be quickly strengthened when danger threatened, as it did when the castle's defences were tested to destruction in war. Residential accommodation would be found at the foot of the castle hill where quite large towns could develop. There would be located the lord's mansion, itself quite modestly defended, while above it towered the wooden superstructure of the *yamashiro*.

Spear

This *kakemono* (hanging scroll) from Ueda Castle shows how samurai warfare was changing during the Sengoku Period. The possession of a horse still tended to indicate a samurai's elite nature – although financial circumstances obliged some to fight on foot – but there had also been a major change in his choice of weaponry.

The mounted archer, once the definitive samurai warrior, was no more. In his place rode the mounted spearman. The 'Way of Horse and Bow' had somehow become the 'Way of Horse and Spear'. We noted earlier the limitations associated with mounted archery, but these restrictions could be set aside as long as warfare was seen as something carried out between one samurai and another. The role then allotted to the warrior's attendants was one of support while the samurai supposedly did all the fighting.

The Mongol Invasions and the Nanbokuchō Wars had shown that the most efficient way of bringing down a mounted samurai was not to use another mounted archer but to set against him half a dozen foot soldiers armed with bows or pole arms. How then, was the samurai to defend himself? His arrows would be at their least effective in such a situation and his sword would have a very limited reach when dealing with foot soldiers, particularly if they were to lure him into the cover of trees and undergrowth.

The answer was to provide the samurai with a *yari* (straight spear) that could be used as a lance or as a slashing weapon as the occasion demanded. By the seventeenth century illustrations of mounted samurai depict the almost exclusive use of *yari* from horseback. Samurai carrying bows are hardly ever illustrated or mentioned in chronicles, and the fact that Shimazu Toyohisa carried one with him at the battle of Sekigahara in 1600 was considered sufficiently unusual for the chronicler to take particular note of it. The shaft lengths varied between 3.2 and 4 metres, while blade lengths varied enormously between about 10 cm and 1.5 metres.

26

Arquebus

鉄砲

The quality of the workmanship that went into making this musket stands in contrast to the simplicity of its firing mechanism.

On the right of the stock is a brass serpentine linked to a spring which drops the serpentine when the trigger is pulled. The serpentine contains the end of a glowing and smouldering match, the rest of which would be wrapped around the stock of the gun or the gunner's arm. To protect from premature explosions the pan into which the priming gunpowder has been carefully introduced was closed by a brass sliding cover that was swung back at the last moment. The explosion in the pan sets off the charge in the barrel with quite a recoil and a lot of smoke.

Simple or not, this type of weapon represents a revolution in Japanese warfare. Arquebuses came to Japan in 1543 when Portuguese traders landed

on the island of Tanegashima and showed the local daimyō these strange new weapons. Tanegashima was owned by the Shimazu clan, and it was to Shimazu Takahisa that the honour went of conducting the first battle in Japanese history at which firearms were used.

Takahisa was one of several daimyō who appreciated the potential of these new weapons, and local swordsmiths, who were already renowned for their metal-working skills, applied themselves to learning the necessary techniques to copy the arquebuses and then mass-produce them. The efficiency and accuracy of the matchlock musket have recently been assessed by means of a series of practical experiments carried out in Japan.

The experiments used Japanese arquebuses made at the beginning of the Edo Period.

The first test was an assessment of the gun's range. Five bullets, each of 8 mm calibre, were fired at a target in the shape of an armoured samurai from distances of 30 metres and 50 metres respectively by an experienced matchlock user.

At 30 metres each of the five bullets hit the target area of the chest, but only one out of the five struck the chest area over 50 metres. Even at 50 metres, however, a bullet that struck home on a man could do considerable damage.

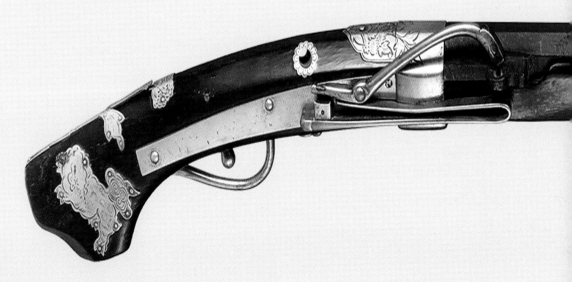

27

Hanging Scroll of Uesugi Kenshin

上杉謙信掛物

This *kakemono* depicts one of the great survivors of the Sengoku Period: the brilliant general and daimyō Uesugi Kenshin (1530-78).

At a time when many minor daimyō succumbed to the pressure of others and the depredations of warfare, Kenshin maintained and increased his petty kingdom until the time of his death. He was devoted to the martial deity Bishamon-ten, and it is the first character of his patron's name that appears on the banner shown in this painting of him. He is also wearing a Buddhist monk's white head cowl, having embraced the life of a monk in addition to his status as a samurai.

Uesugi Kenshin was an opportunist, and even his surname was appropriated because he had no ancestral connections with the ancient family of Uesugi who by 1530, the year of Kenshin's birth, had split into two branches: the Ogigayatsu Uesugi and the Yamanouchi Uesugi. The future Uesugi Kenshin was simply the son of Nagao Tamekage, a retainer of the Yamanouchi branch of the Uesugi.

When Tamekage was defeated and killed in 1536, Kagetora was the strongest of the surviving Nagao children and the best hope for the family's future. Kagetora therefore entered the castle of Kasugayama as his father's heir at the age of nineteen. He was now head of the family, and although all-powerful and well-respected in the immediate area of Kasugayama, he was still only a retainer of the Yamanouchi Uesugi to whom he had sworn allegiance. But while the Nagao prospered the Yamanouchi Uesugi went from bad to worse.

Defeated again and again, in 1551 their leader was forced to seek refuge with his followers. The obvious place was Kasugayama, so Nagao Kagetora agreed to protect his former overlord on his own, very strict terms. Uesugi Norimasa would have to adopt Kagetora as his heir, give him the name of Uesugi and the titles of Lord of Echigo Province and make him Shogun's Deputy for the Kantō area. Norimasa had little choice but to agree to all these demands, so Nagao Kagetora was transformed into Uesugi Kagetora. Kagetora shaved his head and took the clerical name of Uesugi Kenshin in the following year of 1552.

28

Hanging Scroll of Kosaka Masanobu

高坂昌信掛物

Uesugi Kenshin would have been very familiar with the individual shown in this **kakemono** because it portrays one of the leading generals in the service of Kenshin's great rival Takeda Shingen (1521-1573), with whom he fought five battles on the same battlefield of Kawanakajima. Kosaka Danjō Masanobu, one of Shingen's most trusted followers, is depicted as a classic samurai of the sixteenth century. He is wearing a straightforward and practical battledress armour with a complete lack of any unnecessary ornamentation. His face mask is bound tightly within his helmet cords. His sword in slung **tachi** style with a smaller companion sword beside it.

The fourth battle of Kawanakajima in 1561 is illustrated in the smaller picture. The object is an *ema* (prayer board) from the shrine on the battlefield and shows Uesugi Kenshin and Takeda Shingen engaged in single combat. It is evidence of how a great general's plans can sometimes go disastrously wrong. Uesugi Kenshin had advanced deep into Takeda territory and had set up camp on Saijōyama, a mountain overlooking Shingen's castle of Kaizu (modern Matsushiro). Shingen planned to ambush Kenshin. His army would leave Kaizu in secret by night and arrange themselves in battle order on Hachimanbara, the flat plain in the middle of the

Kawanakajima area. Kosaka Danjō's job was to lead a surprise raid up the rear of the mountain on which Kenshin was camped and drive the Uesugi army down in confusion into the waiting ranks of gunners and spearmen.

That was the clever plan, but somehow Uesugi Kenshin became aware of Shingen's night-time manoeuvres and countered with a daring scheme of his own, which was to descend under cover of darkness and attack the Takeda in force while they were still dressing their ranks at Hachimanbara. This they did, so the Uesugi army that came bearing down upon the waiting Takeda were not a fleeing and panic-stricken mob but a full-scale assault that even broke through Shingen's closest bodyguards and allowed the single combat shown here to take place. When Kosaka Danjō reached the summit of Saijōyama the former campsite was of course deserted, so he rapidly headed down the slope to engage the Uesugi from the rear. Through his efforts and those of his fellow generals order was restored and a wholesale defeat was avoided.

29

Wooden Statue of Matsu Hime

松姫木像

Her head is shaved like a man's and her Buddhist robes are wound tightly round her as we contemplate the impassive gaze of a Buddhist nun who was once a proud samurai woman. Matsu Hime was the daughter of Takeda Shingen, and her funerary effigy and certain of her possessions are still owned by the Shinsho-In, the temple in Hachiōji (Tokyo) that received her when she left the samurai world behind. Among the items preserved there is her *naginata*. Like most women of the samurai class there was an outside chance that one day she might have to defend herself, so martial arts formed an important part of her education and the *naginata*, once the preserve of the *sōhei*, was regarded as an ideal weapon for women. Matsu Hime was in fact very good with the *naginata*, although she probably never had to use it in anger, even though her life had been touched by great tragedy.

While still a young girl Matsu Hime was betrothed to Oda Nobutada (1557-1582), the son and heir of Oda Nobunaga, the first of the great daimyō who were eventually to bring order out of the chaos of the Sengoku Period.

Their marriage contract was designed to cement an alliance between the Oda and the Takeda, but the arrangement fell apart completely following the death of Takeda Shingen. Shingen was succeeded by Matsu Hime's brother, the brave yet headstrong Katsuyori.

Disregarding any alliance, even one brought about by his sister's marriage, Katsuyori took up arms against Oda Nobunaga and was heavily defeated at the battle of Nagashino in 1575. Takeda Katsuyori then withdrew to the security of his territory within the mountains of Central Japan and it took seven more years of campaigning for Oda Nobunaga to destroy him. The final battle happened in 1582, and after the conflict Matsu Hime was informed

that her brother had been killed by her father-in-law.

Later in that same year a further disaster struck. Oda Nobunaga was resting in the Honnōji in Kyoto when he was subjected to a surprise night attack by one of his own generals, Akechi Mitsuhide. Mitsuhide had chosen his moment carefully. Most of Oda Nobunaga's army were engaged in a military campaign in the west of Japan. Mitsuhide was supposed to be joining them, but as he left Kyōto he wheeled his army round and attacked instead the temple where Nobunaga was defended by only a small bodyguard. They were unable to defend him against the treacherous attack so Nobunaga committed suicide.

The Akechi men then sought out Nobunaga's heir Nobutada (Matsu Hime's husband) and killed him too, so within one year Matsu Hime had lost her husband, brother and father-in-law. Seeking only to withdraw from the world she entered a convent and never returned.

Itagaki Nobukata's War Fan

板垣信方の団扇

Communication was very important on a Japanese battlefield, and the starting point for any signal transmitted down the chain of command would be the waving of the commanders's *dansen* (war fan). His subordinates would be watching anxiously to see the fan being lowered to indicate the launch of an attack and its overall direction, a sign followed within a split second by the leaders of the individual units. The man holding this fan is one of Takeda Shingen's 'Twenty-four Generals' Itagaki Nobukata (1489-1548), who was killed at the battle of Uedahara.

There were several different types of war fan. One, shown later in this book, consisted of a number of oiled paper tassels hanging from a shaft. Others were made exactly like a lady's fan that opened and closed but differed by having the spines made of iron. Nobukata's fan is like a large version of a sumo referee's baton and has painted on it a representation of the constellation of the plough. Made from iron or lacquered wood it could also act as a small defensive shield, and Takeda Shingen is believed to have defended himself using his fan when Uesugi Kenshin broke into his lines at Kawanakajima.

Uedahara came about when the Takeda troops were exhausted after a long march in cold weather but attacked the Murakami army with their customary gusto in a classic Takeda mounted advance. Itagaki Nobukata led Shingen's vanguard as the Murakami absorbed the Takeda charge within their ranks and surrounded them. Nobukata died fighting. Shingen himself was involved in the hand-to-hand spear fighting and was wounded in his left arm, but the fight eventually became a stalemate as the two sides settled down in prepared positions. After twenty days no fighting had resumed, so Takeda Shingen withdrew to Kōfu and Murakami Yoshikiyo let him go. Some 700 Takeda soldiers had died at Uedahara and one chronicle records that 'the grief in the province was unending'.

One fascinating detail about Uedahara is the use by Shingen's enemy Murakami Yoshikiyo of simple short-barrelled Chinese hand guns as a response to the devastating power of the Takeda cavalry. The difference between their use and the Portuguese arquebuses, introduced to Japan only five years before Uedahara, is illustrated by Murakami's orders to his gunners to fire the guns, discard them and use their swords. The days of organised firearm squads had not yet arrived, but Murakami's willingness to experiment shows that he was a leader to be reckoned with.

An *ashigaru's okegawa-dō*

足軽の桶側胴

The prominent hole in the front of this simple breastplate could have been produced by the test firing of an arquebus, but it may also conceal a very ominous story.

In the absence of any other information we may surmise that its wearer was killed instantly by a massive gunshot wound to the chest produced by a large calibre bullet that went straight through the iron plates. There is no *mon* (family badge) to indicate the man's affiliation, but we may safely conclude from the fact that he was wearing a simple type of armour known as an *okegawa-dō* that he was an *ashigaru* (foot soldier) The name literally means 'light feet', a reference to their use as light troops in contrast to the well-armoured mounted samurai, rather than a suggestion that they might run away from a battlefield. That had certainly been common in the early days when *ashigaru* were acquired by casual temporary recruitment and the promise of loot, but the more astute generals gradually realised that they could be transformed into organised and ordered weapons squads wielding bows, spears and in particular the weapon for which organised squads were most appropriate: the matchlock arquebus.

One of the most important developments in samurai warfare during the sixteenth century was the imposition of discipline and organisation on these lower class warriors who were issued with simple uniform suits of armour. The plain *okegawa-dō* style shown here had a breastplate consisting of several iron plates riveted together and lacquered. It is on show at the museum of the battle of Sekigahara and may have been worn at that famous struggle in 1600.

This thought-provoking object echoes the findings of the experiments noted above that tested the arquebus's power. Bullets of 9mm calibre were fired at ranges of 30 and 50 metres against wooden boards and iron plates.

At 30 metres each was pierced cleanly. At 50 metres the bullet entered the 48 mm board for three quarters of its depth and also entered a 2mm iron plate, causing a dent on the inside, but not passing through. As the iron from which the scales of a typical armour of the Sengoku Period were made was of about 0.8 mm thickness such armour could be holed by a bullet fired at 50 metres, and this may well have been the fate of our anonymous *ashigaru*.

32

Painted Screen of the Battle of the Anegawa

姉川合戦屏風

Oda Nobunaga was the first of the unifiers of Japan, and the battle of the Anegawa (the Ane River) was one of his most impressive victories. The painted screen of the battle shown here is owned by Fukui Prefectural Museum.

Although only painted in 1837 it is superbly executed in the traditional style. The artist clearly carried out considerable research before painting it, including a meticulous attention to detail of the heraldry of the opposing sides. It includes several interesting vignettes of incidents that happened during the battle, which came about as a result of an advance by Nobunaga against his brother-in-law Azai Nagamasa. Nobunaga drew up his army in a defensive formation, where he rested and waited for reinforcements. Azai Nagamasa, meanwhile, received support from Asakura Yoshikage. Nobunaga had the advantage of numbers, but some of his troops were of doubtful reliability because they been levied for service from lands which had previously belonged to the Azai. The reliable Toyotomi Hideyoshi was put in charge of this questionable contingent. Help also arrived from Tokugawa Ieyasu. Oda Nobunaga had originally intended that the Tokugawa troops should attack the Azai, but Nobunaga bore Nagamasa a personal grudge, so he resolved to oppose Azai himself.

The battle began at 04.00 hours. As it was summer, the sky was already light and as the day wore on the sun climbed higher and blazed down on to the two armies. The overall impression is of a huge hand-to-hand melee in the middle of the shallow river. At first it was almost as though there were two separate battles being fought: the Tokugawa against the Asakura, and the Oda upstream against the Azai. Both sides waded into the river, which flowed slowly and was about one metre deep. The sweat poured off the samurai and mingled with the waters of the river, which were soon stained red. On the left of the screen Tokugawa Ieyasu is shown in his field headquarters. His *tsukai-ban* (courier guards) some on foot, others mounted, go about their vital business of carrying messages as the fighting ebbs and flows across the river. In one of those bold strokes of which he was master, Ieyasu sent his second division under Honda Tadakatsu and Sakakibara Yasumasa on to Asakura's flank. This action is shown in the top centre of the screen, as horsemen under Honda (shown by his *mon* of hollyhock leaves) sweep across.

At this point there occurred a splendid example of samurai heroism. It was essential that the Asakura army withdrew to the northern bank, and a samurai called Magara Jūrōzaemon Naotaka volunteered to cover their retreat. His action is shown in the centre of the screen. Jūrōzaemon was a giant whose preferred weapon was an extra long *no-dachi* sword. His challenge was first accepted by a vassal of Ogasawara Nagatada, whom he killed. He was then joined by his eldest son Magara Naomoto, and together father and son faced repeated attacks by Tokugawa samurai. Gradually the Asakura army managed to disengage itself and pull back across the river while the two brave men followed slowly, swinging their huge weapons in wide circles and lopping off arms and legs. It took a simultaneous attack by four samurai to defeat them.

Jūrōzaemon met the first with force and swung the enormous sword which cut his opponent on the thigh, then with a second slash knocked the helmet off his head, smashing it to the ground. He then cut through his spear. At this the man's younger brother ran to his assistance, and was met by a vicious sweep to his side. Yamada Muneroku, a veteran warrior sixty years old, lost his weapon when his spear shaft parted under a blow, leaving one only to join in the fray. He was armed with a cross-bladed spear, and managed to hook one of the cross blades under Magara's armour and haul him from his horse to the ground. Magara was quickly decapitated. His son tried to withdraw to the Asakura army while attempting to avenge his father, but was met by a samurai who introduced himself and engaged him in fierce fighting, at the end of which the younger Magara was killed. Their sacrifice had not been in vain, because their rearguard action had allowed the army to rally, even though they were then pursued for a considerable distance.

33

The War Drum of Hamamatsu Castle

浜松城陣太鼓

The Mitsuke School Building in Iwata (Shizuoka Prefecture) owns an unusual object in addition to its displays about Meiji Period education. The object is a war drum.

On the battlefield or from the ramparts of a castle, the stirring sound of the war drum would encourage samurai into action, but the Iwata drum is a very special one because its sound prevented a defeat from being turned into a disaster. In 1572 the beating of this drum within the gate tower of Hamamatsu Castle guided the losing army home and fooled the enemy into thinking that they had not really won.

The drum call was the final act of the battle of Mikatagahara, a mighty showdown between the well-established power of Takeda Shingen and the future Shogun of Japan Tokugawa Ieyasu (1542-1616). The headstrong young general was determined to stop Shingen's advance into his territory by battle rather than a long siege, and it had been reported to him that the Takeda army was drawn up in full battle order on the high ground of Mikatagahara just to the north of the castle. The Tokugawa army marched out of the safety of Hamamatsu at about four o'clock in the afternoon as the snow was beginning to fall. Aware of their approach, Takeda Shingen took up a strong defensive position from which the advancing Tokugawa could be enveloped.

The Takeda cavalry were not charging a defensive line as they would do at Nagashino three years later. Instead they were advancing against disordered troops, and very soon the Tokugawa army was in full retreat. Hoping to mislead the Takeda, Natsume Yoshinobu, the commander of Hamamatsu Castle turned back to the enemy lines shouting 'I am Ieyasu!' and plunged into the fight to be killed. In a further attempt at deception Ieyasu sent to the castle a samurai who had cut the head

from a warrior wearing a monk's cowl which he falsely claimed to be the head of Takeda Shingen, but the trick gave them only a temporary respite from worry when the rapid arrival of Ieyasu made it appear that defeat was certain.

The castle commander was just giving orders for the gates to be shut and barred when Ieyasu interrupted him. To shut the gates was precisely what Takeda Shingen expected them to do, he reasoned. Instead Ieyasu ordered the gates to be left open for their retreating comrades and huge braziers to be lit to guide them home. To add to the confident air Sakai Tadatsugu was sent up into the tower where the large war drum was installed and began beating it loudly.

As Ieyasu had predicted, when the Takeda advanced to the castle and saw the open gates and heard the drum they immediately suspected a trick. They also noted that the Tokugawa dead who had died in the advance lay face downwards, while those killed in the retreat lay on their backs. None had turned his back to the enemy. The Tokugawa samurai were men to be reckoned with, so no night-time assault was made on the vulnerable castle.

If the Takeda had known the truth about how weakly Hamamatsu was actually defended they could have taken it by assault, but Takeda Shingen decided to withdraw to his mountains and return the following year, rather than risk a winter siege of Hamamatsu, which an all-out attack may well have taken it. So the whole Takeda army pulled back, fooled completely by the Tokugawa resolve and the beating of the drum.

34

Torii Sune'emon

鳥居強右衛門

When a battle flag bears upon it an image of someone being crucified the obvious conclusion will tend to be drawn. This remarkable flag shows a man on a cross, but there is no connection with Christianity. The figure is Torii Sune'emon (1540-75) the hero of the battle of Nagashino, Oda Nobunaga's most famous victory.

Sune'emon was serving in the garrison of Nagashino Castle when it came under siege by Takeda Katsuyori in 1575. He volunteered for the almost suicidal task of leaving the castle to request help. He swam down the Toyokawa until he reached the nets which the Takeda had strung across it, cut a hole in the net under the water without making a sound, swam through, and continued on his way. At dawn on 24 June he lit a beacon as a pre-arranged signal to inform the garrison that he had managed to get through and then carried on to Okazaki. He reported that the castle had by then only about three days supplies of food left and that when that had gone all that the commander could do was to offer to commit suicide to save the lives of his men. Oda Nobunaga and Tokugawa Ieyasu promised to move the next day.

Torii Sune'emon then began the hazardous journey back to the castle to let the garrison know that help was on its way. Unfortunately for him the Takeda had seen the beacons. They spread sand on the river bank to disclose footprints and rigged up bells on ropes across the river, so Torii Sune'emon was caught and brought before Takeda Katsuyori. Katsuyori heard his story, including the intelligence that a relieving force was on its way, and offered Sune'emon service in the Takeda army. Torii Sune'emon apparently agreed, but the suspicious Katsuyori insisted that he demonstrate this change of allegiance by addressing the garrison and telling them that no army was on its way and that they should surrender Because Katsuyori did not trust Sune'emon he was tied to a cross.

As Katsuyori had feared, instead of urging the defenders to surrender he shouted to them to stand fast. One account tells of spears being thrust into his body as he uttered these words, others of his execution later. However or whenever he died, many in the Takeda army were moved by his example. One retainer called Ochiai Michihisa was so impressed that he had this flag painted. The smaller picture shows the well-known end of the battle of Nagashino, when the terrific charge of the Takeda cavalry that had triumphed at Uedahara and Mikatagahara was finally broken by Nobunaga's use of volleys of gunfire.

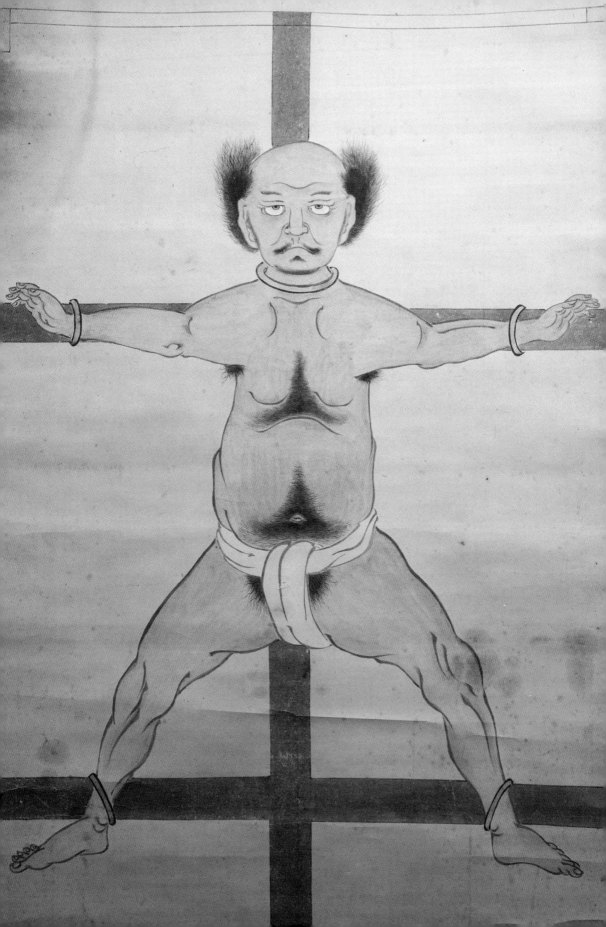

35

Battle Standard in the Form of a *gohei*

御幣馬印

Japanese heraldry differed from European heraldry in one particular visual form, because in addition to the use of a flag as a battle standard samurai armies would go into action beneath great three-dimensional battle standards called *uma jirushi* (literally 'horse insignia'), the most spectacular sight on any battlefield. Shibata Katsuie (1530-1583) used this *uma jirushi* made in the shape of a Shintō priest's *gohei*, a paper-on-wood baton used for giving blessings.

The standard was made from wood and lacquered gold. At one of Katsuie's battles it was lost to the enemy, and Katsuie's retainer Menju Ietora risked his life to retrieve it, an incident shown in the smaller illustration.

By the early seventeenth century most daimyō would have two *uma jirushi*: a great standard and a lesser standard. They were sometimes large rectangular flags, but were more usually these huge three dimensional objects, often made from wood, in the shape of bells, umbrellas, gongs or streamers. Tokugawa Ieyasu was known for his large golden fan with a red rising sun, while Oda Nobunaga used a large red umbrella. Toyotomi Hideyoshi used a gold-lacquered gourd shape as his standard in recognition of his bravery at the siege of Inabayama in 1564. He had led a detachment of men up a narrow mountain path, and they signalled to Oda Nobunaga's troops waiting below by waving their water gourds from the end of their spears.

The final form of Hideyoshi's standard was the striking 'thousand gourd standard', last flown in battle by his son Hideyori at Osaka in 1615. It had many (although by no means a thousand) golden gourds, each representing one of his victories. Other daimyō chose objects that had personal significance to them. Konishi Yukinaga, who led the invasion of Korea in 1592, was the son of a medicine dealer from Sakai, so for his *uma jirushi* he displayed a huge white paper bag as used by pharmacists in Japan, with a large red sun painted on it. The Ōmura of the Nagasaki area used a huge golden bell, while Ankokuji Ekei, who had once been a Buddhist monk, sported a large golden lantern.

36

Stone with the Face of a Devil

鬼石

Apart from a few carved blocks of stone covering the fragments of its earthen base, this carved stone with a devil's face is all that has survived of Kitanoshō Castle in Echizen Province (modern Fukui Prefecture), the seat of Shibata Katsuie, which suffered total destruction in 1583.

Katsuie, shown in the smaller picture, had been one of Nobunaga's most loyal generals, but when Nobunaga died there was a dispute over who should succeed him. It was the talented and astute Toyotomi Hideyoshi (1536-1598) the future unifier of Japan who eventually came out on top, and one of the victories that secured his position as Nobunaga's heir was the battle of Shizugatake against the advanced troops of his former comrade-in-arms Shibata Katsuie, the commander of Kitanoshō Castle.

Shizugatake was an isolated frontier castle belonging to Hideyoshi and was under

siege from Sakuma Morimasa. Shibata Katsuie was very concerned about how vulnerable Morimasa was to a rear attack. Toyotomi Hideyoshi was apparently fully occupied with a siege of Gifu Castle, but the prudent Katsuie sent a messenger to Sakuma Morimasa ordering him to abandon his open siege lines for the security of newly captured Ōiwa castle. Sakuma Morimasa pooh-poohed the idea; Shizugatake would be his prize before night fell, and he dismissed out of hand any suggestion that Hideyoshi could return to its relief when he was tied up outside Gifu. So Sakuma disobeyed the orders of his commanding officer and stayed fighting. Six times Shibata Katsuie sent the order, and six times Sakuma refused to comply.

Very early in the morning of 20 April 1583, Toyotomi Hideyoshi left 5,000 men to continue the siege of Gifu and began the great gamble. The only way he could achieve surprise was by taking a largely mounted army with him while the infantry and supplies marched along far behind. It was an enormous risk to separate the different units of his army in this way, but it was a chance that Hideyoshi had to take. His army of 1,000 mounted samurai and their exhausted personal attendants hurried along the familiar and well-trodden road, and the first that Sakuma Morimasa knew of their arrival was the sudden appearance

of 1,000 burning pine torches down in the valley. Then, following a signal from a conch shell trumpet blown, it is said, by Hideyoshi himself, his eager and impatient men poured up the mountain paths.

When the first of Sakuma's retreating troops came hurtling down into the valley and along the road north to Kitanoshō Castle Shibata Katsuie realised that the day was lost. It was a hopeless situation, but he had done his duty. When the third and second baileys of the castle fell Shibata Katsuie retired to the keep with the members of his family and resolved to go to his death in spectacular samurai fashion. The keep was filled with loose straw which was set on fire, and Shibata Katsuie committed *seppuku* among the flames. The devil's head stone is all that remains.

Cannon of Ōtomo Sōrin

大友宗麟の大筒

Kunikuzushi ('the destroyer of domains') was the name once given to two of these cannon, Ōtomo Sōrin's secret weapon.

This full-sized reproduction is mounted within Usuki Castle, from where Ōtomo Sōrin Yoshishige (1530-87), the daimyō of Bungo Province (modern Ōita Prefecture), defied the mighty Shimazu of Satsuma. Sōrin is remembered as one of the most prominent daimyō to have accepted Christianity as a result of the preaching of the Portuguese Jesuit missionaries who were active in Japan from 1549 onwards. He was baptised in 1578 and took the name of Francisco.

In 1586 the Shimazu advanced upon Sōrin's castle of Usuki as part of their campaign to take over the whole of Kyushu. The Shimazu vanguard advanced to a position where woods concealed their final movements, but within the castle great hopes were laid on the Portuguese breech-loading cannons, which had been obtained because of the Ōtomo's impeccable Christian connections. At Usuki Castle two were being used to defend a fortress for the first time.

They were heavy bronze swivel guns, which means that the trunnions rotated vertically within a swivel-yoke bracket that was itself mounted to rotate horizontally. A *kunikuzushi* was also a breech-loader, because instead of being rammed down

the muzzle the ball, powder and wad were introduced into the breech inside a sturdy chamber shaped like a large tankard with a handle. A metal or wooden wedge was driven in behind it to make as tight a fit against the barrel opening as could reasonably be expected, and the gun was fired. The main disadvantage was leakage around the chamber and a consequent loss of explosive energy, but this was compensated for by a comparatively high rate of fire, as several breech containers could be prepared in advance.

The *kunikuzushi* were mounted near the main gate on the dedicated stone gun platform shown here, Japan's first such structure. The cannon were fired and the shots hit the grove of willow trees where the Shimazu troops lay concealed, and soon many dead and wounded Satsuma samurai lay beneath the splintered branches. The Shimazu were shaken by this unexpected development, but regained their composure sufficiently to mount an assault. This was beaten off, and soon the operation deteriorated into a stalemate. We may presume that the cannon were used many times, because eventually the Shimazu withdrew, shaken by this new military technology.

Battle Map of Tanaka Castle

田中城の陣取図

In 1990, while archaeological investigation was under way at the site of Tanaka Castle in Kumamoto Prefecture, a local scholar decided to search the archives of the Mōri family, whose ancestors had been involved in the epic siege of Tanaka in 1587. The researcher had hoped to find some written references to the little known battle, but a chance find surpassed anything he had expected, for hidden among the family's papers was Japan's oldest battle map.

It shows Tanaka under siege and provides a unique snapshot of a samurai battle. The footpaths up the castle hill are shown as lines and the division into *kuruwa* (baileys) is delineated very well using exaggerated slopes. The fences are drawn as a series of sharpened wooden stakes linked together and just below the top are a number of symbols in the shape of the Greek letter *pi* to indicate barracks for the soldiers. The besiegers' palisade is prominently drawn and is shown crossing the river at two places. There are twelve gateways to allow the entry of attacking parties. The map also confirms the names of the besieging commanders and the layout of their troops in a number of linked cartouches. Written just outside the cartouches are the distances from the castle where their units were stationed expressed in multiples of *chō* (109 metres).

Over a period of thirty-eight days the Wani family defended Tanaka against 10,000 troops sent by Toyotomi Hideyoshi. The desperate and ultimately doomed defence of the castle by one-tenth of that number was a heroic act of defiance, but for centuries its story remained as little-known as scores of other similar operations.

The map and the archaeological excavation have changed all that, and in addition to the details noted above it provides one other piece of intriguing information. Tanaka's southern *demaru* (a projecting area akin to a European ravelin) included an open work wooden tower (*yagura*) that has been confirmed by archaeological excavation. It is most unlikely that the tower would have been built by the defenders because it would have given them no advantage over the field of view available from their own towers in the baileys and would have been a useful prize for the enemy. It must therefore have been built by the besieging army under fire.

The sacrifice in lives when building it would have been considered worthwhile because the finished *yagura* would have allowed Hideyoshi's army to fire into the inner baileys on an almost level trajectory. It also enables us to pinpoint the stage in the siege at which the map was drawn. Rather than being a static depiction of the siege lines therefore, Japan's oldest battle map is in fact a snapshot of an important moment of decision because it shows the plans for the final assault on the castle, after which Tanaka sank into obscurity for 400 years.

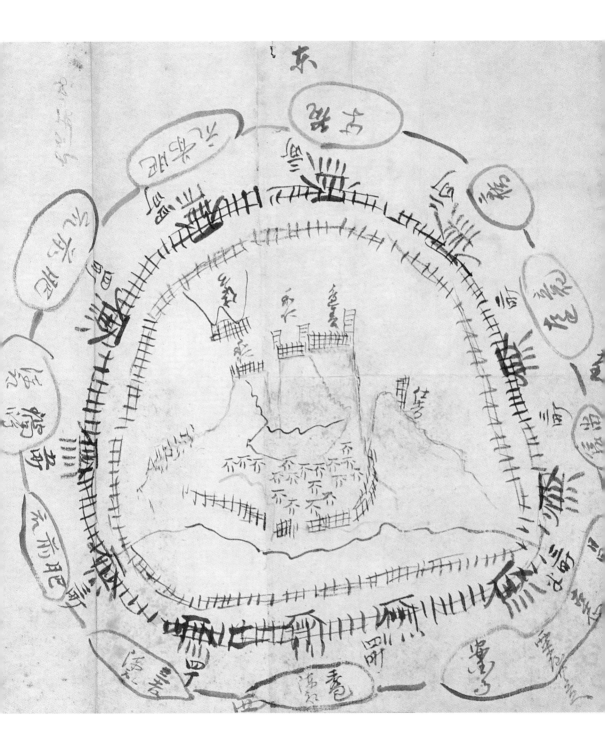

39

The Kai Shrine and Yufu Korekiyo's Grave

甲斐神社と由布惟清の墓

Samurai, the bringers of death, are not usually associated with healing, but there are two examples in Kumamoto Prefecture where a samurai deified after his death as a _kami_ has acquired some association with healing or the prevention of illness.

Both men were involved in the military campaign that included the siege of Tanaka Castle. The Kai Shrine in Kumamoto City enshrines Kai Sōryū, a samurai who was killed during the attack on Kumamoto Castle in 1587 after his arms and legs were cut and incapacitated. The main _kami_ of the Kai Shrine is Ashite Kōjin the _kami_ of the

limbs, and because of the circumstances of the death of Kai Sōryū he is worshipped there along with Ashite Kōjin. Replicas of hands and legs are offered to both _kami_ by people seeking healing of the limbs, while a few designated wooden specimens that clearly possess great powers are rubbed on to the affected part of the body by the petitioner. By these means the powers of Ashite Kōjin and Kai Sōryū are brought to bear on the illnesses associated with the parts of the body of which they are _kami_.

The other picture shows the grave of Yufu Korekiyo, a samurai who became a _kami_ of the ears after his death at Tanaka. Towards the end of the final attack on the castle its commander Wani Jinki had resolved to meet a heroic death, and his resolve to perish gloriously was matched by an equal determination on the part of the besiegers to be the one who took his head.

Yufu Korekiyo, a retainer of the Tachibana, was one of them, but a samurai called Tsuda Yohei was the first to gallop up and confront Jinki, who slashed back at him with his sword and cut the man almost in two from the peak of his helmet to his groin. Jinki then received a challenge from Yufu Korekiyo. Jinki was stationed at the North Gate and when Korekiyo rode off his

followers suspected that he might be heading into danger and called out to him to return, but Korekiyo was deaf so did not hear them. As they feared one of the defending archers, who was acting as a sharpshooter and was concealed from view, loosed an arrow at him.

It pierced Korekiyo's breastplate and went through as far as the middle of his back. He fell dead from his horse.

Yufu Korekiyo's grave lies to the south-east of the castle site among a grove of bamboo. Because of his deafness and its influence on the manner of his death he is enshrined as a *kami* of the ears, and offerings are made to his spirit in the form of piles of *hifukidake*, short tubes of bamboo that have a small hole through a node at one end. They are traditionally used for blowing life into a smouldering fire. Thus did a fierce warrior become a god of the deaf.

40

The Red-Walled Temple

赤壁寺

The outside walls of most Buddhist temples in Japan are usually painted white or cream, but the Gōganji in Nakatsu (Ōita Prefecture) is different. Its walls are red and they tell a savage story, because the red colour was supposedly chosen to hide bloodstains that could never be removed.

The temple was built by Kuroda Yoshitaka (1546-1604), who took a prominent part in Hideyoshi's invasion of Kyushu in 1587 and was granted six districts of Buzen Province (Fukuoka Prefecture) as a reward. His takeover produced a backlash from the dispossessed landowners of Buzen. Their leader was Utsunomiya Shigefusa, who attacked Yoshitaka's castle at Nakatsu. Much of the fighting took place in the nearby temple district and the blood of the slain samurai splattered on to the white walls of the Gōganji. After the battle it was repainted, but the bloodstains always showed through, so eventually it was painted red.

The other memorial to Utsunomiya Shigefusa is the Shiroii Shrine which is within the grounds of Nakatsu Castle. It is somewhat unusual to have a shrine within one's castle that enshrined the spirit of a dead rebel, but after Shigefusa's death he became that most terrible of things: an angry ghost. A persistent Japanese belief states that when a person dies a violent or untimely death he remains possessed by the worldly passion in which he died. Vengeful spirits such as these (often dead samurai slaughtered on battlefields) provide rich material for the numerous ghost stories and plays that make up many Noh and Kabuki dramas. In a vivid metaphor, the spirit at the time of death had sharp edges and still retained a strong individual personality. If the proper rituals were carried out it gradually lost its sharp edges and became as smooth as marble, eventually losing all its individuality as part of the collective spirits of the locality.

The battle of Dannoura in 1185, which ended so tragically for the Taira, was to result in almost an entire family of unhappy spirits roaming the earth searching for revenge. One other notorious angry ghost was Taira Masakado, who was enshrined in the Kanda Myōjin shrine in Tokyo after a series of floods, droughts and epidemics had been blamed on his unruly spirit. Shigefusa was just the same.

Kuroda Yoshitaka retired in 1589 and passed Nakatsu Castle on to his son Kuroda Nagamasa who was the first to be haunted by the angry ghost of Utsunomiya Shigefusa, so the shrine was built to placate his spirit. Shigefusa now sleeps in peace, as did the successive owners of Nakatsu Castle, even though the vivid red walls of the Gōganji still reminded them of the deaths their ancestors had once brought about.

41

Bronze Statue of Bernardo Nagasaki

ベルナルド長崎銅像

During the Sengoku Period many daimyō started out as samurai who rose to power based on their accomplishments and their victories. Hōjō Sōun, for example, emerged from obscurity to found a dynasty, while Tokugawa Ieyasu's descendants would rule Japan for two and a half centuries. Nagasaki Jinzaemon Sumikage achieved neither of these things. His skills were in diplomacy and the art of avoiding conflict, so no Nagasaki dynasty ever grew to dominate Japan. Instead he gave his name to one of Japan's greatest cities.

The port city of Nagasaki lies on the western coast of Kyushu in an area divided geographically by huge complicated inlets, islands and forested capes. It was a place where minor daimyō could prosper in small isolated communities, and for many years the territory of Nagasaki Jinzaemon Sumikage was just such a place. He converted to Christianity and took the name of Bernard (Bernardo), but like so many other small daimyō he was eventually forced by circumstances to enter into vassalage with a powerful neighbour. In his case the new overlord was Ōmura Sumitada (1533-87), the first and most passionate of all the Christian daimyō, who had ordered that the whole of his domain, comprising some 60,000 souls in all, should become Christian. Mass baptisms followed, accompanied by the destruction of Shinto shrines and Buddhist temples.

Bernardo Nagasaki fought for the Ōmura against their many rivals until 1580 when the anti-Christian Ryūzōji seemed about to overwhelm them. At this point the cautious Bernardo urged negotiation. Ōmura Sumitada had other ideas, for which

Bernardo Nagasaki had unwittingly provided a precedent. In 1570 Bernardo had effectively pawned his lands to the Jesuit missionaries in return for a temporary loan to buy weapons.

In 1580 Ōmura Sumitada went much further. He was now in control of Nagasaki and knew that the Jesuits were looking for a secure base where Portuguese ships could safely trade. Nagasaki, being a 'long cape' (*naga saki*) was ideal, so in return for money and arms Sumitada donated the future port city to the Jesuit Order. It was a deal without precedent in Japanese history because Nagasaki then became something unique on Japanese soil: a European colony in all but name. The terms of the gift specified that the Jesuits had full jurisdiction over it, and within two weeks of the agreement plans were being laid for Nagasaki to be fortified.

By the end of 1581 Nagasaki had been surrounded by a rammed earth wall and wooden palisades and armed with a few small cannons formerly sent as presents to Ōmura Sumitada. Portuguese families were

encouraged to settle in Nagasaki, and were told that in times of attack they would be invited into the shelter of the fortifications.

Yet within six years the Jesuit colony of Nagasaki would swallowed up along with all the Christian daimyō of Kyushu when Japan's southern island was conquered in the massive military campaign by Toyotomi Hideyoshi. Unlike all his other new territories Hideyoshi did not pass Nagasaki on to one of his followers, and it was to stay under government control as a vital port and gateway to the outside world, retaining the name of Bernardo Nagasaki, the minor lord who had once owned it.

42

Katō Yoshiaki

加藤嘉明

The samurai are not commonly thought of as sea-going warriors but some daimyō were as much lords of the sea as they were lords of the land, and in Katō Yoshiaki (1563-1631) we have an excellent example of a samurai admiral.

This is not to say that Yoshiaki's achievements were always seaborne. He first made his name in 1583 when he was feted as one of the 'Seven Spears' of the battle of Shizugatake. Yoshiaki went on to become one of Toyotomi Hideyoshi's admirals but was present at Japan's greatest naval defeat.

Toyotomi Hideyoshi is sometimes referred to as the Japanese Napoleon because his tactical and strategic vision was similar, as was the loyalty he inspired in his senior officers, but like Napoleon he also overreached himself on one huge and disastrous campaign. By 1591 Hideyoshi had brought the whole of Japan under his control, and the following year he turned his attentions towards invading China, for which a route up the Korean peninsula was the most practical course.

Katō Yoshiaki was one of the men placed in charge of the naval side of the operation, and at first all went well for the expeditionary force as they mounted a blitzkrieg attack that took them swiftly to Seoul. The Korean king fled north, but the Japanese advance stalled when a Chinese army crossed the border and the Korean navy started breaking their lines of communication.

Katō Yoshiaki then had to take on Korea's admiral Yi Sunsin. Katō Yoshiaki, Wakizaka Yasuharu and Kuki Yoshitaka were given the task of seeking out Yi Sunsin to destroy him. Wakizaka's fleet was ready, but neither Katō nor Kuki had enough time to assemble the number of ships they felt they needed for the operation. Being eager for personal glory, Wakizaka decided to act alone instead of waiting until they all were ready. Yi decided to try a false retreat to lure the Japanese out to the south-west, where a wide expanse of sea fringed by several uninhabited islands would provide an ideal location for a sea battle.

The bait was taken, and from the north-east came Yi's vanguard, beating down the straits with the entire Japanese fleet in hot pursuit. When the Japanese were well clear of the rocky strait and out into the sea around Hansan Island they found Yi's main body waiting for them. With Yi's famous armoured 'turtle ships' as the vanguard the Korean fleet rowed towards the focal point of their formation. Cannon were fired and the fight became a bloody free for all, the Korean ships trying initially to keep their chosen victims at a distance so as to bombard the Japanese without the risk of a boarding party being sent against them.

Hardly a single ship escaped and countless numbers of Japanese were hit by arrows and fell dead into the water. By this time Katō Yoshiaki and his colleague were well on their way, and Yi met them at Angolp'o. Katō did not respond to a false retreat so Yi changed tactics and sent in relays of

ships to bombard the Japanese as they lay at anchor. Much damage was caused, but he eventually pulled back, fearing that if the Japanese were forced to land they would take revenge on the Korean villagers nearby. So Yi let Katō Yoshiaki escape, well satisfied that the Japanese enemy had lost command of the sea.

43

Konishi Yukinaga

小西行長

In this print from _Taiheiki Eiyū den_ Konishi Yukinaga, the leader of the invasion of Korea in 1592, contemplates the severed heads of his enemies.

Born probably in 1558 in Kyōto, he was baptised as Augustin and prospered as a merchant, negotiator and general, placing each role at the disposal in turn of Oda Nobunaga and Toyotomi Hideyoshi. Yukinaga eventually acquired the fief of Shōdojima, a large island in the Inland Sea from where he could combine his naval expertise and business acumen in a way that greatly benefited Hideyoshi's expansionist plans.

Konishi Yukinaga acquired Higo Province (now the southern part of Kumamoto Prefecture) in 1587. The territory included the staunchly Christian Amakusa Islands, but Yukinaga's personal espousal of Christianity did not necessarily mean that his new subjects welcomed him with open arms. Indeed, Yukinaga's Christianity may well have been the only positive thing they could find in his favour, and great animosity developed when Yukinaga ordered them to supply corvée labour for the building of his castle at Uto. Juan Amakusa Hisatane and Juan Shiki Rinsen both refused to comply. On 31 October 1589, showing no particular sympathy towards his fellow Christians, Yukinaga despatched a general called Ijichi Bundayū against them with 3,000 troops, but Rinsen caught and massacred them. Yukinaga then led a large army against Rinsen's castle of Shiki, where the defender's Christian connections had provided him with a bonus in the form of Portuguese cannons. They enabled him to put up a spirited defence that lasted eight days.

Meanwhile, Yukinaga's anti-Christian ally Katō Kiyomasa began a bitter siege of Hondo Castle. The desperate nature of the defence allowed Kiyomasa to make little immediate impression on it, so Konishi Yukinaga had to bring reinforcements. While he waited in the siege lines for an order to follow into the attack Katō Kiyomasa began a major assault on New Year's Day 1590. The Jesuit Luis Frois stresses the Christian devotion displayed by the defenders, who made their confessions to the priests before going into battle. His image of the fathers granting absolution inside the church as stray bullets whizzed past their heads is a very vivid one. He also notes that women took part in the fighting.

Katō Kiyomasa's troops soon broke into Hondo Castle and a massacre began. Augustin Konishi Yukinaga appears to have taken no part in the fighting until he was requested by Katō Kiyomasa to attack the back gate, but he delayed his assault to give the Christian defenders time to escape. Augustin Konishi's career did not suffer from his act of mercy. Hideyoshi in fact approved, but the enmity it caused between him and Katō Kiyomasa was to cause problems when their dislike of each other erupted into disagreement over strategy during the invasion of Korea in 1592.

小西攝津守
行長

賣小西清兵衛後
父ハ泉州堺の商
始め弥九郎と云
如清と号ハ行長
備前
岡山の商人の
養子となる
其性富
撰那の辯
あるを以て澤田
直家京師の使者
奇才を賞し後其
の役に清正と倶に
先駈して
その功を伯仲せり

44

The Siege of Haengju

幸州大捷

This bas relief at Haengju Castle in Korea shows one of the decisive Korean actions against the Japanese that would eventually persuade the invaders to go home. In an action that had passed into legend even the women of the garrison played their part, carrying stones to the front line in their aprons and their skirts. The fortress lies not far from Seoul and was commanded by Kwŏn Yul, the outstanding Korean general whose statue stands on the site.

Haengju overlooks the Han River and covers all the approaches down to the capital. On hearing of the Japanese advance Kwŏn Yul strengthened its fortifications with ditches and palisades and waited for his opportunity.

At dawn on 14 March 1593, Ukita Hideie led a massive 30,000-strong Japanese army out of Seoul to crush the minor annoyance. Konishi Yukinaga and Kobayakawa Takakage are two of the famous names who took part. The attack began about 06.00 with little overall plan, just a steady advance up the steep slopes of Haengju from all directions, but the Koreans were waiting for them. Dug in behind earthworks and palisades they replied with bows, arquebuses, delayed action mortar bombs, rocks and tree trunks.

Pride of place in the Haengju armoury, however, were a substantial number of the curious armoured artillery vehicles called hwach'a (fire wagons). A hwach'a consisted of a wooden cart pushed by two men on level ground, or four on steep ground. On top of the cart was mounted a honeycomb-like framework from which either 100 steel tipped rockets or 200 thin arrows shot from gun tubes could be discharged at once.

Timing was of course crucial because a hwach'a could not be easily reloaded, but the Japanese attack at Haengju was delivered in the form of dense formations of men marching slowly up a steep slope, so conditions could hardly have been better.

Nine attacks in all were made against Haengju, and each was beaten off for a total Japanese casualty list that Korean sources claim may have reached 10,000 dead or wounded. After the battle, notes Yi Sŏngnyong in Chingbirok, 'Kwŏn Yul ordered his soldiers to gather the dead bodies of the enemy and vent their anger by tearing them apart and hanging them on the branches of the trees.' With Haengju undefeated, the long Japanese retreat began.

45

Armour of Kobayakawa Takakage

小早川隆景の具足

This suit of armour is part of the most complete example outside Japan of a samurai's full ensemble or *omote dōgu*.

The equipment in its original form is believed to have been presented by Toyotomi Hideyoshi to Kobayakawa Takakage (1532-1596) as a reward for his service in Korea. As well as this fine armour the collection includes weapons, textiles and horse furniture. It was extensively remounted during the eighteenth century.

The style of body armour is a *nuinobe-dō*, made from six scalloped iron plates and laced in light blue silk. The helmet is set off with fine gold fittings. Behind the seated figure is a longbow and a quiver full of arrows.

Kobayakawa Takakage's service came to its height when the Japanese retreated from P'yŏngyang to Seoul in 1593. A few days before the siege of Haengju began Takakage mounted a desperate rearguard action at Pyŏkjeyek, which proved to be the biggest land battle of the war and resulted in the triumphant Chinese general Li Rusong being driven back northwards in disgrace. Yet in spite of the heavy Chinese losses it did nothing to change the overall strategy and the Japanese retreat from Seoul was delayed by only a few days.

Pyŏkjeyek was a fierce hand-to-hand fight where the razor sharp edges of the Japanese blades cut deep into the heavy coats of the Chinese and Japanese foot soldiers tugged mounted men from the backs of their horses using the short cross blades on their spears. It is unlikely that Takakage ever wore the armour shown here in battle, because he died in 1596 just before the second invasion of Korea began. The statue of him is on the site of his final domain: Mihara on the Inland Sea.

46

Statue of a Siamese War Elephant

サイアムの戦象銅像

One little known aspect of the history of the samurai is the military service they provided overseas. Japanese mercenaries were recruited from three different sources: the **wakō**, from emigrant and refugee Japanese communities and by direct recruitment within Japan itself.

The first country to make use of them was China, but from the late sixteenth century onwards the rulers of Siam and Cambodia courted their services, and the earliest surviving written record of Japanese mercenaries fighting anywhere in Southeast Asia is to be found in Siam at the battle of Nong Sarai in 1593. This was the epic struggle celebrated to this day in Thailand where King Naresuan of Siam not only drove back a Burmese invasion but killed the Burmese Crown Prince in a single combat from the back of an elephant. A unit of Japanese samurai fought from war elephants, and an account of the Japanese contingent at Nong Sarai appears in the *Royal Chronicles of Ayutthaya* as: 'Phra Sena Phimuk, mounted on the bull elephant Füang Trai and in command of the corps of 500 Japanese volunteers', perhaps the least well-known of any battle in which samurai took part.

The European colonial powers also employed Japanese warriors as mercenaries, but there was a considerable difference in how they were regarded. The Southeast Asian kings tended to employ samurai on a long-term basis as palace guards while European employers usually hired them on a temporary basis for specific campaigns.

We may also discern a profound difference in attitude towards them, because the Southeast Asian monarchs tended to place long-lasting trust in their Japanese mercenaries while the Europeans showed little expectation of continuing loyalty. That may have been because mercenaries in contemporary Europe were notoriously fickle, but the European commanders who had charge of Japanese mercenaries often had underlying suspicions that such reckless warriors might even rise up against their masters. In short, the Europeans admired the mercenaries but they also feared them, so that in every case a shift in attitude may be discerned from initial enthusiasm to great suspicion that the Japanese might one day turn against them, either from within the expatriate communities or even by invasion from Japan.

Matsumoto Castle

松本城

By the end of the Sengoku Period the Japanese castle had evolved into the form with which we are familiar today, and this miraculous survivor from 1597, the tower keep of Matsumoto Castle, is one of the finest examples.

The earlier model of living quarters in a valley combined with a lookout tower on a hill had become merged into one massive complex where the mountain itself had disappeared under a maze of intersecting stone bases, towers, walkways, parapets and gatehouses. It would be crowned by a splendid multi-storey keep that allowed a commanding view of the daimyō's territory and provided a crucial visible symbol of his power. More mundanely, it also provided a solid last-ditch refuge in times of war should every other tower and courtyard of his castle have fallen to an enemy.

Like other examples, Matsumoto is built on top of a massive stone base. Although usually referred to as 'walls' this is a somewhat misleading term to use because the bases were produced less by building 'up' than by building 'on', as thousands of workmen followed a precise geometric pattern to clad in stone the slopes of existing hillsides.

The bare surfaces were precisely smoothed to produce a pre-arranged slope that would combat erosion, add strength and provide a secure base in which the downward thrust resulting from the weight of the superstructures would be directed outwards. The solidity of the bases provided a good defence against earthquakes, but their real strength was not to be illustrated until as late as 1945, when the atomic bomb took away Hiroshima castle's keep in an instant but left the stone base virtually untouched.

A typical castle keep like Matsumoto would be of at least three storeys, maybe even as many as seven, but frequently their outward appearance did not correspond exactly to their actual interior structure and design because there were often underground cellars built deep inside the stone core of the base and the number of floors above ground was often not discernible from the apparent number visible from outside. Unlike almost anywhere else in the castle, the windows, roofs and gables of the keep were arranged in subtle and intricate patterns. The shape of the keep's roof was almost without exception in the ornate style that had been used for centuries for the most palatial residences, and the use of two contrasting styles of gable on the same elevation of a keep was also a frequently noticed aesthetic element. This style of architecture can be seen to good effect at Matsumoto.

Painted Screen of the Siege of Ulsan

ウルサン籠城屏風

Hideyoshi's armies returned to Korea for a second invasion attempt in 1597. This time the reverse was much swifter in coming and the Japanese were soon forced back to the line of *wajō* ('Japanese castles') which they had built along the coast at the end of the first invasion.

Ulsan was Japan's last *wajō* to be constructed and was still unfinished when a Ming army attacked it in the epic siege of 1598 illustrated on this painted screen made originally for the Nabeshima family. Thousands of Chinese soldiers are climbing up the walls in what became almost the final action of the disastrous Korean expedition.

Having been advised by their scouts that the Japanese defences were still incomplete, a Chinese flying squad was sent on ahead of the main body to do as much damage as possible, and because some of the gates were still missing the Chinese were able to swarm inside the outer baileys and began loosing fire arrows from outside the walls. They were eventually driven back, but at the cost of 660 Japanese casualties. Katō Kiyomasa could only wait for reinforcements, hoping that the awful weather might help in persuading the Chinese to withdraw. The Ming set up siege lines to starve out the defenders and watched all the approaches by land and sea in case of a relief attempt. Terrifying assaults were delivered regularly over the next ten days.

As one furious surge of men was driven back another wave swept up to replace it, the dead bodies of their predecessors taking the place of scaling ladders as they clambered up the huge mound of corpses. As Ulsan had no well within the inner castle the torments of thirst were soon added to the intense discomfort of the fierce Chinese attacks. Water-gathering parties slipped out of the castle by night and brought back supplies from ponds choked with corpses.

When the temperature dropped below freezing and a strong wind arose it brought

about a wind-chill factor so severe that it affected the fighting spirit on both sides. By now all food was exhausted except for roasted strips of meat cut from dead horses cooked over fires made from broken arrows, piles of which lay several feet deep. Foraging parties had been reduced to searching the bodies of dead Chinese for grains of rice. The exhausted soldiers huddled in the sunny places on the ramparts and fell asleep, only to freeze to death in the shadows. Two days later a

large Japanese relieving army arrived nearby and the Chinese withdrew.

The smaller picture shows Kiyomasa noting the flocks of scavenging birds descending on the abandoned Chinese lines. Three other Chinese advances against Japanese positions followed later in the year, but before these operations were fully under way Toyotomi Hideyoshi died peacefully in his sleep. The Japanese armies were recalled and the Korea invasion was over.

49

The Fujito Rock

藤戸石

Garden design is one of Japan's greatest cultural achievements, but the one seen here hides a sad story.

Toyotomi Hideyoshi was a great patron of the arts and the Sanbō-In in Kyōto houses one of his favourite temple gardens. Among the numerous rocks that help make up its extraordinary miniature landscape is the prominent one to the left of the photograph. It is said to have been stained by the blood of a victim of samurai warfare. Hideyoshi had particularly coveted it even though it was in someone else's garden. His powers of persuasion were such that the Fujito Rock was immediately transferred to Sanbō-In to become the central feature.

The innocent blood was shed in 1185 during the final campaign of the Gempei War. The two Minamoto brothers Yoshitsune and Noriyori were harassing the Taira towards their eventual end at the battle of Dannoura. Yoshitsune's victory at Yashima is well known, but while he was earning military glory in a spectacular fashion his younger brother was conducting a comparatively unglamorous campaign against the Taira along the coast of the Inland Sea. Noriyori's objective was to control the Straits of Shimonoseki where the Taira had their main base. He would then cross over to Kyushu and take up a position in the Taira rear, but because of the Taira command of the sea the coastal advance had to be carried out overland and the Taira naturally harassed him at every

turn. Noriyori defeated one of these thrusts at the battle of Kojima, also called Fujito (in modern Okayama City).

The Taira felt quite secure in their small fortress in the sea but Sasaki Moritsuna, one of the Minamoto commanders, did some investigating. He realised that the low tide might reveal a passable causeway, which he confirmed through a local fisherman, whom Moritsuna first rewarded and then killed lest his valuable intelligence be revealed. At dawn the following morning, 10 January 1185, Moritsuna led his horsemen across the shallow waters. The Taira outpost was overrun, but Noriyori's force did not have any boats with which to pursue the Taira as they put to sea.

The combination of daring and callousness shown by Sasaki Moritsuna at Kojima would provide much future artistic inspiration. The Noh play *Fujito* has Moritsuna returning to the site of his triumph to be confronted by the dead fisherman's grieving mother and then by the ghost of his victim. More quietly dramatic is the Fujito Rock at the Sanbō-In. When Moritsuna murdered the fisherman his blood spilt on to this large 1.8 metre high stone, which stands today as a curious but very moving memorial of the true horrors of samurai warfare.

50

The Bloody Ceiling of the Hōsen-In

宝泉院の血天井

The ceiling of the Hōsen-In in Ōhara near Kyōto was once the floor of a castle's keep, and the dark stains, blackened with age, come from blood shed during a mass act of ritual suicide in the year 1600.

The incident came about following the death of Toyotomi Hideyoshi in 1598. Japan had split once again into warring factions. On one side were the supporters of Hideyoshi's infant heir. On the other was Tokugawa Ieyasu. In 1600 conflict started between the two sides and Ieyasu was soon forced to move north to deal with a threat to the Tokugawa lands from rivals in Tōhoku. It was very important to each side that the strategic castles they owned should be retained and rival castles captured, and the most important of these was the Tokugawa possession of Fushimi to the south of Kyoto.

The siege of Fushimi proved to be one of the most decisive actions of the campaign that finished with the battle of Sekigahara. It was under the overall control of Torii Mototada and among the garrison were over 100 samurai from Kōka in Ōmi Province. No impression was made upon the fiercely defended fortress so Natsuka Masaie, lord of the castle of Minakuchi, seized the wives and children of two of the Kōka samurai while their menfolk were absent.

An arrow letter was loosed into Fushimi, informing them that if they cooperated by setting fire to the castle they and their followers would be richly rewarded. If they refused their wives and children would be crucified.

In order to save them the wretched men agreed. They persuaded forty of their followers to join them, set fire to a tower and took down a section of the wall. The enemy broke in and after much desperate fighting Fushimi fell with a huge loss of life including all of the Kōka contingent who had still remained loyal. They had however inflicted considerable losses upon their enemies and also bought precious time that Ieyasu was able to exploit at the decisive battle of Sekigahara.

Torii Mototada did his heroic best to save the castle after treachery had betrayed it. Eventually, with his followers reduced to ten, he sat down on a step to rest for a moment from his exertions. When an enemy samurai challenged him Mototada announced his identity and the assailant waited respectfully to take his head while Mototada and his followers committed suicide. Greater respect was shown later, because the floor on which they committed *seppuku* was now soaked in their blood with red hand prints that spoke of the tragedy. After the battle of Sekigahara the floor was carefully removed and sections from it now form part of three 'bloody ceilings' at temples around Kyōto.

51

Painted Screen of the Battle of Sekigahara

関ケ原合戦屏風

Tokugawa Ieyasu's hour of destiny can be summed up in one word – Sekigahara – where, on a foggy October morning in 1600, he fought one of the most decisive battles in Japanese history.

This detail from a painted screen of the fighting at Sekigahara shows Shima Sakon of the anti-Tokugawa coalition known as the Western Army charging into battle. The battlefield itself appears in the smaller picture.

It was a dark and damp evening when Ishida Mitsunari, the leader of the Western Army, marched out to take up a position from which to oppose Ieyasu's advance. On the hills around stood field defences surrounded by ditches and palisades. Ieyasu marched straight ahead, relying first on his loyal followers to absorb whatever punishment that the Western Army could give them, but gambling most on the assurance he had been given that certain of Ishida's followers intended to change sides once the battle had begun. The most important among these was Kobayakawa Hideaki, whose role as Ishida's second wave for a flank attack would be crucial. The Eastern vanguard engaged Shima Sakon, Gamo Ujisato and Konishi Yukinaga in a massive and indecisive series of melees.

A second wave of Easterners brought fresh impetus to the attack on Konishi Yukinaga, whose formation began to collapse. It was time for Ishida Mitsunari to bring into action the large force on his right wing to deliver

the decisive blow to the Tokugawa eastern flank. This was Kobayakawa Hideaki stationed on Matsuoyama, which was a considerable distance away. It had been agreed that he would join the battle when he saw the plume of smoke from a signal fire lit above Ishida's headquarters. The fire was ignited, but there was no movement on Matsuoyama. Horseback messengers were sent to him but still no reinforcements materialised. Tokugawa Ieyasu, meanwhile, was also becoming concerned, because the assurance he had been given was not

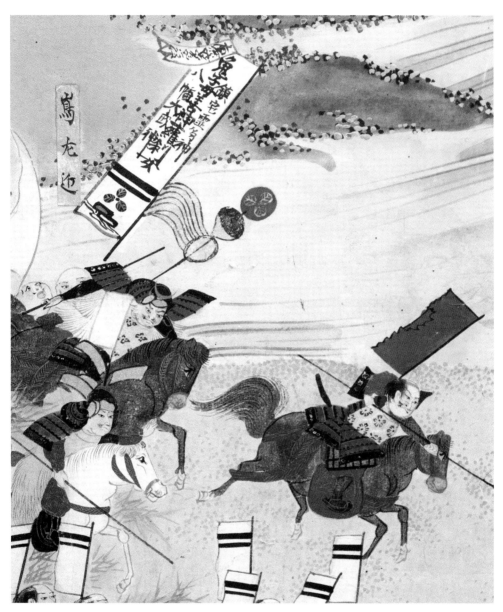

merely that Kobayakawa would do nothing but that he would actually change sides. So Ieyasu ordered his men to open fire on Kobayakawa's position.

This proved to be the decisive stimulus he needed and his troops started to descend Matsuoyama and move across to attack their former comrades. By 14.00 hours, Ieyasu was sufficiently confident that the day was his that he began to prepare for the head-viewing ceremony, so he took off the light cloth hood that he had been wearing and put on his helmet for the first time in the battle. The memory of the death of his former overlord Imagawa Yoshimoto in similar circumstances forty years earlier must still have been a vivid one, so his comment 'After a victory tighten the cords of your helmet' was to become a Japanese proverb.

Red Armour of the Ii Family of Hikone

彦根赤具足

Of all the ways in which one might enhance one's army's appearance on the battlefield the prize must surely go to the Ii family of Hikone in Ōmi province (modern Shiga Prefecture), who dressed all their troops in brilliant red. This became their own unique 'red badge of courage' in the already colourful world of samurai heraldry. This helmet with large golden *kuwagata* ('antlers') is an excellent example.

The Ii had been vassals of Imagawa Yoshimoto until the battle of Okehazama put paid to all the Imagawa ambitions. When rumours grew within the Imagawa household that their vassals were planning to abandon them a purge of the Ii followed. The sole survivor was the 3-year-old Naomasa, who had been born in 1561.

Somehow he survived under the care of his aunt, and lived for the next few years in the protection of the temple where she was a Buddhist nun. By the early 1570s the Imagawa had lost all their lands after repeated attacks from their neighbours, so Ii Naomasa emerged from his hiding place to claim his fortune. It was important for him to ally himself with a successful local daimyō if he was to have any chance of success, and one fortunately presented himself in the shape of Tokugawa Ieyasu.

From that moment on the fortunes of the Ii began to flower. In 1576 Naomasa is credited with saving Ieyasu from an assassination attempt and in 1581 he helped capture the castle of Takatenjin by draining off the water supply.

Along with grants of rice lands Ii Naomasa also received the service of many of the Takeda's old retainers who were absorbed into the Tokugawa army after the defeat. Among these samurai were the troops who had fought for Yamagata Masakage, the renowned veteran Takeda general who had been killed at Nagashino. He was the younger brother of Obu Toramasa, who had dressed all his samurai in red armour. Tokugawa Ieyasu suggested that Ii Naomasa should copy the practice, so the Ii *aka sonae* (red regiment) was born. They fought with distinction at Sekigahara and Osaka.

Armour of Tachibana Muneshige

立花宗茂の具足

The old castle town of Yanagawa preserves many memories of the Tachibana family, and this spectacular suit of armour set off with black cocks' feathers that was once owned by Tachibana Muneshige is one of its prize possessions.

Tachibana Muneshige (1567-1642) was a supporter of Ishida Mitsunari's Western Army and therefore an enemy of Ieyasu. Before Sekigahara he had led a successful attack on Ieyasu's castle of Ōtsu at the narrow neck of Lake Biwa. After the loss of Fushimi Ōtsu was the only Eastern possession near Kyōto and was held stubbornly by Kyōgoku Takatsugu. The Tachibana attack began on 19 October and was successfully concluded on 21 October, the day of the Battle of Sekigahara which completely negated the achievement. One fascinating detail about the siege of Ōtsu is that the local people climbed the hill behind it to watch the fighting from a safe distance.

After the defeat at Sekigahara Tachibana Muneshige fled back to Kyushu and his castle of Yanagawa to seek refuge. Ieyasu sent after him Nabeshima Katsushige, Kuroda Jōsui and Katō Kiyomasa, and the resulting military action was to provide a unique example of a variation on the familiar theme of warrior monks in the person of Ginchiyo, the warrior nun of Yanagawa. The castle's defence was helped by the presence of a small defended strongpoint to the south in the shape of the convent where Tachibana Muneshige's divorced wife, Ginchiyo, now resided. In an act of surprising loyalty to her ex-husband Ginchiyo organised her fellow nuns in armed resistance against the advancing army of Katō Kiyomasa.

We know very little about the actual defensive measures adopted by Ginchiyo. Her resistance may only have been one of dressing up in armour and looking defiant, but it seems to have made the point. Kuroda and Katō proposed that Tachibana Muneshige should surrender and join them in a campaign against the Shimazu, who had also fled from Sekigahara. Muneshige agreed, but Ieyasu ordered the campaign to stop almost before it had begun because he did not want a further war in Kyushu. Tachibana Muneshige was then pardoned and stayed as daimyō of Yanagawa, where his fine armour has remained to this day.

54

Statue of Arima Harunobu

有馬晴信木像

Dignified in the frozen pose of his funerary effigy in Maruoka (Fukui Prefecture), the territory of which he was the daimyō, sits Arima Harunobu (1567-1612). Although popularly celebrated as one of the great Christian daimyō Harunobu's conversion had been very opportunistic.

Upon inheriting the lands from his father Yoshisada in 1576 Harunobu had embarked upon a persecution of the numerous Christians who had followed Yoshisada's example of baptism. It was only when Harunobu found himself in desperate straits as a result of aggression by his neighbour Ryūzōji Takanobu that Harunobu also accepted baptism in return for generous military support from the Jesuits. Receiving the Christian name of Protasio, Harunobu applied himself with equal zeal to the persecution of any remaining pagans. His positive contribution was the founding of the Arima seminary, the Jesuits' first formal educational institution in Japan.

Harunobu's moment of fame came in 1609 when he was commissioned by the Shogun to send an armed expedition to Taiwan. The aim was to secure Taiwan as an intermediate trading base for China, thus circumventing the Ming ban on trade. The expedition was officially commissioned, well-planned and run on strict military lines, but in spite of all the preparations Arima's men found no central authority with whom to make contact either for diplomacy or for war. Instead of meeting a king (as they had supposed) they were attacked by aboriginal headhunting tribesmen.

The samurai fought back and then prudently withdrew. In an acknowledgement of Ieyasu's orders they took some aborigines prisoner and transported them back to Japan. These unfortunates were presented to Ieyasu, who soon realised that he was not dealing with ambassadors, so the Taiwanese were given presents and allowed to return home.

A further unsuccessful attempt to annex Taiwan was tried in 1616, after which Japan left it alone.

55

Samurai and Cherry Blossom

武士と桜花

He sits astride his horse, his commander's war fan in his hand and with his back to the castle of Ōgaki that he owned.

Toda Ujikane is every inch a samurai, and to complete the picture he is framed by cherry blossom, the most poignant symbol of the samurai's life. It can also be a symbol of the samurai's death when the fallen petals represent bodies on a battlefield, as shown in the smaller picture from Aizu-Wakamatsu Castle.

During the eighth century the Japanese aristocracy had sought two things within the cultural sphere: to embrace the best of Chinese civilisation and to give it a uniquely Japanese flavour. So whereas the Chinese prized the plum blossom, the Japanese grew to love the cherry blossom. *Hanami*, the ritualised viewing of the flowering trees that is so popular even today, began at this time. With the rise of the samurai the cherry blossom acquired another level of symbolism because it was seen to represent the fallen warrior.

The samurai's life was brief and evanescent. Like the cherry blossom he flowered for but a short while and died at his moment of greatest beauty. Asano Naganori, the daimyō whose forced suicide led to the famous vengeance of the Forty-Seven Rōnin, composed a farewell poem comparing himself to a cherry blossom, writing, 'Sadder than the blossoms swept away by wind/a life torn off when spring is in its fullness'. Many centuries later the Japanese soldiers sent overseas to fight for the emperor were told that they would die for their sovereign like beautiful falling cherry blossom.

Nowadays the flowering of the cherry blossom is appreciated and enjoyed in Japan in a completely peaceful manner, and it is only the sight of samurai like Toda Ujikane wreathed in these flowers that remind the onlooker of the long association made between them and the noble doomed samurai.

56

The Ehon Ryūkyū Gunki

絵本琉球軍記

Ehon Ryūkyū Gunki is the title of an illustrated woodblock printed book that tells the story of one of Japan's very few successful overseas military expeditions.

In 1609 the independent kingdom of Ryūkyū, the group of islands which now form the Japanese prefecture of Okinawa, was subjected to a rapid, fierce and brilliantly executed raid on the Shogun's behalf by Shimazu Iehisa, the daimyō of the province of Satsuma, whose family had maintained a legal claim to the Ryūkyū archipelago for many centuries. *Ehon Ryūkyū Gunki* is a clever piece of Satsuma propaganda.

The Shimazu were Japan's great survivors. In 1587 they were crushed by Hideyoshi but allowed to retain their ancestral lands. At Sekigahara in 1600 they were again on

the losing side and fled ignominiously from the battlefield, but were then spared the massive programme of transfer of territories whereby almost all the other daimyō were moved about like so many potted plants. Tokugawa Ieyasu had looked at the geographically distant Satsuma and saw the advantages of leaving them to rule the remote but strategic area of Japan that they knew so well.

The subsequent operation against the Ryūkyūs was designed to demonstrate the Shimazu's loyalty to the Tokugawa. It consisted of a series of armed landings

along the chain of islands, the establishment of a secure beachhead and then a two-pronged advance by land and sea against the main harbour of Naha and the royal palace at Shuri. Within a matter of days King Shō Nei was a prisoner and 250 years of control by Satsuma had begun.

Satsuma's pride in the fact that its army of only 3,000 had captured a kingdom was to be romantically depicted in *Ehon Ryūkyū Gunki*, with dramatic woodblock pictures by Okada Gyokuzan (1737-1812), who had previously illustrated *Ehon Taikōki*, a fictionalised life of Hideyoshi. The main picture shown here depicts Shimazu Iehisa ready to depart for the Ryūkyūs. Iehisa sits under two battle standards, each of which have the cross-shaped *mon* of the Shimazu, but the artist Okada Gyokuzan has played

a trick on his patrons. The picture is in fact a reworking of an illustration from the earlier *Ehon Taikōki* that showed Toyotomi Hideyoshi watching his fleet leaving for Korea. The original is shown on the opposite page. Not only has the caption been changed, but also the heraldry on the battle standards. Hideyoshi's 'thousand gourd' standard has been replaced by the Shimazu device and the Toyotomi paulownia *mon* has given way to the cross.

The technique was quite simple. Each spread of the books was printed from a separate carved wooden block, so the author's assistant has carved the old area away with his chisel and glued in a replacement with the new words or pictorial details. Military deception could clearly work at very different levels!

57

Nakijin Gusuku

今帰仁グスク

Gusuku was the name for a castle on the Ryūkyū Islands, and when the Shimazu of Satsuma attacked Okinawa in 1609 King Shō Nei placed great faith in these unique stone fortresses.

Most were built in positions overlooking the sea and covered the approach to harbours, like this one at Nakijin. The *gusuku* were nothing like Japanese castles. Their walls were not solid bases enclosed in stone that had been carved out of a mountain, but castle walls that would have been more recognisable as such to a European visitor. Although resembling Korean and Chinese walls in many respects, they did not always follow the contours of a hill like the Great Wall of China. Instead they enclosed successive baileys on a hillside in which were administrative buildings made from wood. The sweeping walls of Katsuren Gusuku are shown in the smaller picture.

In its heyday Nakijin was the largest of the *gusuku*. It was built on a natural defensive position with a sharp cliff dropping to the Shikema River on its eastern side, dense forests to the south and the sea to the

north. Low parapets along the tops of the walls provided the only protection for soldiers stationed along them, making them even more vulnerable to attack than the walls around Korean cities that had fallen so rapidly in 1592. The only superstructure along the walls was above the gateways, the castle's strongest points of defence. The northern one was the Heiromon, which provides the entrance for visitors to Nakijin today. The stonework has been carefully restored, showing the gun ports on either side of the entrance which provide the evidence of the early use of firearms by the Ryūkyūan kings. These early guns would have been short-barrelled Chinese varieties, but heavier weapons would have been mounted in them in 1609. Additional wooden structures would have consisted of a lookout tower above the gateway, probably with a thatched roof, and very heavy gates within the stone portals.

58

Silver Catfish Tail Helmet of Maeda Toshinaga

前田利長の銀鯰尾兜

Samurai generals loved elaborate helmets. This one was owned by Maeda Toshinaga (1562-1614), and as the accompanying photograph of the statue of his father, Maeda Toshiie (1538-1599), makes clear, a taste for tall dramatic helmets ran in the family.

Toshiie's golden helmet is in the style known as 'elongated courtier's cap', being based on the *eboshi* that was worn by noblemen attending the emperor. Toshinaga's silver helmet represents the tail of the catfish and makes an allusion to the giant catfish that was believed to cause earthquakes, so that the approach of the Maeda army would be like an advanced warning of an earth tremor!

In 1551 Maeda Toshiie had become a page to Oda Nobunaga, and in 1556 his stipend was tripled after he suffered a wound in his right eye. In 1562 Toshiie was made a member of Nobunaga's elite Horse Guards and soon became acquainted with the area of Japan that he would one day make his own.

The provinces of Echizen and Kaga, which lay to the north of Kyōto, were hotbeds of the Ikkō-ikki, the fanatical lower class Buddhist armies who fought as confederacies and despised the daimyō. 1575 Nobunaga attacked Fuchu in Echizen (modern Takefu) and wrote two letters from the site. One contained the chilling

116

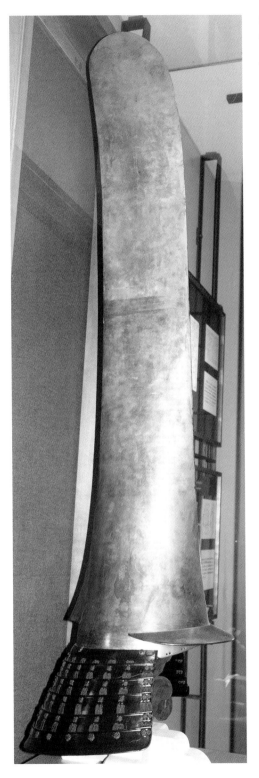

sentence, 'As for the town of Fuchu, only dead bodies can be seen without any empty space between them.' Maeda Toshiie's personal involvement in the slaughter has recently been dramatically confirmed by an archaeological find, because an inscribed tile found on the site of Komurayama Castle in Echizen records his name along with the date and the number of prisoners executed. Toshiie went on to serve Hideyoshi, who doubled the size of the Maeda domain.

He also instructed Toshiie to move his headquarters to Kanazawa which was to be the Maeda centre for the next 300 years, but in 1584 Sassa Narimasa attacked Toshiie's castle of Suemori.

A painted scroll made to commemorate the battle of Suemori shows the Maeda father and son in these tall helmets at the battle.

It was Toshinaga who led Maeda troops to Korea while Toshiie directed affairs from Japan. When Hideyoshi was near to death in 1597 Maeda Toshiie was one of the five regents he appointed to support Hideyoshi's infant son Hideyori and to assume the affairs of government until he was of age. Toshiie died peacefully in 1599 and Toshinaga succeeded him. Although he did not take part in the battle of Sekigahara he kept Ishida Mitsunari's allies busy elsewhere in Japan.

For this the Maeda were generously rewarded, and their final wealth would be assessed as 1,250,000 *koku* of rice. One *koku* was the amount that was theoretically needed to maintain one man for one year. It meant that in size and power the Maeda family stood second only to the Tokugawa.

Toshinaga had reason to be grateful to his talented father, who had risen from pageboy to daimyō.

59

Namban Helmets of the Tachibana Family

立花家の南蛮兜

Row upon row of golden lacquered helmets adorn the corridors of the Ohana, the former mansion of the Tachibana daimyō in Yanagawa. They are of simple construction and have an unusual shape, because they are 'namban', or Southern Barbarian', helmets.

This derogatory expression was applied to the European visitors who had begun arriving in the 1540s.

Although Europeans were often treated with suspicion and would eventually be expelled from Japan, certain aspects of the Western culture they brought along endeared them to the Japanese rulers.

The introduction of firearms is their best known military innovation, but the Spanish morion helmet also aroused interest. It was made from beaten iron and provided a useful alternative to the conventional

Japanese helmet bowl. Neck guards in the Japanese style could easily be added.

These examples associated with the Tachibana also reveal an interesting social phenomenon, because sporadic crazes for European fashions could flourish even during times of persecution against the unwelcome Western import of Christianity.

Hideyoshi, who was responsible for the first Christian martyrdom in Japan, liked wearing a rosary and was keen on European food. Tokugawa Ieyasu is supposed to have worn a helmet like these at the battle of Sekigahara along with a sturdy Spanish body armour. These mass-produced Tachibana helmets would have been seen on the heads of the family's *ashigaru*, making their army look like an array of Spanish conquistadors!

60

The Uto Tower of Kumamoto Castle

熊本城の宇土櫓

Augustin Konishi Yukinaga, the invader of Korea, went on to choose the losing side at Sekigahara. He was captured there and executed shortly afterwards on Tokugawa Ieyasu's orders. Following his elimination Katō Kiyomasa took over most of the Konishi fief in Southern Higo and made Kumamoto the main castle for the province.

Kumamoto's original Uto Tower is shown here. Yukinaga's Uto Castle had been completely destroyed and for centuries it was popularly believed that its main tower was dismantled and moved to Kumamoto. Recent research, however, has established that the name is derived instead from the offices located inside it where officials administered Konishi's former territories.

Whatever their aesthetic appeal, Japanese castles were primarily fortresses. The Japanese castle represented a sophisticated defence system, even if the way this operated is not always directly apparent. At first sight the graceful superstructures look flimsy and very vulnerable to fire, but they were in fact highly fire resistant and the Japanese also lacked the means for effective artillery bombardment until quite late in their history. One obvious disadvantage provided by the gently sloping and curved walls of the typical castle stone base was the ease with which attackers could climb them, and the way in which the blocks of stone fitted together also provided numerous handholds. One solution was the incorporation into the design of towers of

ishi otoshi (stone-dropping holes) akin to European machicolations. They were closed by hinged doors. At Kumamoto castle the first storey actually overhangs the stone base so as to give a rectangular shape, and the extra space created was used to provide an area for dropping stones. An additional deterrent to would-be climbers were rows of spikes pointing downwards such as are also seen on the keep at Kumamoto.

Considerations concerning food supplies were a very crucial point, and the strangest device for combating starvation may be found at Kumamoto castle. Katō Kiyomasa had suffered the bitter personal experience of the siege of Ulsan, so not only did he plant nut trees within Kumamoto's baileys, but the straw *tatami* mats that are to be found in every Japanese dwelling were stuffed not with rice straw but with dried vegetable stalks, so that if the garrison were really desperate they could eat the floor! Kumamoto's strength was tested and passed when it came under siege during the Satsuma Rebellion of 1870. The castle was assaulted by modern weapons and held out.

122

Battle Standard in the Form of a shakujō

錫杖馬印

A spectacular *uma jirushi* in the form of a *gohei* was shown earlier, and now we have one of the most unusual *uma jirushi* of all. It was used by the Tsugaru family from the far north of Japan, who fought under this gigantic *shakujō*, a priest's staff.

A *shakujō* was essentially a metal 'rattle' made from six rings attached round a frame. It was traditionally carried by the itinerant *yamabushi* priests to frighten away dangerous animals while they were on their mountain pilgrimages.

The larger varieties of *uma jirushi* like this were very heavy and often unwieldy to

carry, but there does not appear to have been any equivalent Japanese device resembling the standard-bearing cart that was used in contemporary Italy. Instead painted screens show a human standard bearer with his master's *uma jirushi* strapped to his back in a specially strengthened holder. The man would steady the contraption using two long ropes, and in the case of the largest types more ropes would be held by two other foot soldiers. It is known that some daimyō deliberately recruited sumo wrestlers as standard bearers because of their immense strength. The *fukinuki*, which were huge streamers rather like the devices in the form of a carp used at the Boys' Festival, were particularly difficult to manage in a high wind because they filled up like a windsock.

Tsugaru Tamenobu, whose name was previously Ōura, submitted to Hideyoshi who confirmed him in the possession of his territories in 1591 and gave him the name of Tsugaru. His son Nobuhira (1586-1631), the owner of this *uma jirushi*, followed his father and built the castle of Hirosaki (Aomori Prefecture), one of the few fortresses in Japan to have survived intact. A small *shakujō* appears on the front of his helmet as a crest.

Miyamoto Musashi

宮本武蔵

A certain madness is perhaps indicated by this picture of the famous Miyamoto Musashi, the greatest wandering swordsman of all.

Musashi's life has been so obscured by legend and fiction that it is difficult to disentangle the real man from the myth. He comes over as a strange character, solitary and obsessive, whose skills with the sword were unquestioned and greatly admired, but which at the same time made him feared and disliked. He also seemed to have an aversion to personal cleanliness. He seldom changed clothes and almost never took a bath, which was very unusual for a Japanese person. Nowadays his taste for violence would probably lead to him being classified as a psychopath.

In 1605 Musashi set off on a *musha shugyō* (warrior pilgrimage) and fought some sixty authenticated duels over the following eight years. In Kyōto he defeated two brothers from the Yoshioka family, having first used a little psychological warfare by arriving late for each contest and thereby unnerving his opponents. He fought the elder with a *bokutō* (wooden practice sword) and knocked him unconscious, breaking his right arm. The younger took up the challenge with a long sword but Musashi killed him using his own normal-sized *katana*. Disgraced by this reverse, the surviving Yoshioka brother issued a further challenge, but he was planning an ambush, not a sword fight.

The scheme was that as soon as Musashi was engrossed in the duel the other Yoshioka followers would attack him *en masse*, and avenge their previous reverses. But their tongues wagged a little too freely, and Musashi got to hear of the plot. So when he arrived at Ichijōji in northern Kyōto, the venue that had been selected, he was prepared for the sudden rush of swordsmen that descended upon him. The attackers were put off by his unexpected composure, and their careful plan went to pieces. One by one they fell beneath Musashi's sword.

Miyamoto Musashi's life also involved short periods of service to various daimyō, numerous duels, and an increasingly deep philosophical insight into swordsmanship which took its final form in the famous *Gorinshō* (The Book of Five Rings) which he completed shortly before his death in 1645. He was also very skilled at painting, thus showing the deep intellectual side of Japan's most famous killer.

63

Nimai-dō Armour of King James I

二枚胴具足

For centuries the giving of gifts has oiled the wheels of international diplomacy, and Japan is no exception. This armour was a gift for King James I of England (VI of Scotland) by the Shogun Tokugawa Hidetada (1579-1632) and was taken to England in 1614.

It was a token of the serious negotiations that had been taking place since the time that England's East India Company had turned its attentions to Japan. That had happened in 1613, when Captain John Saris sailed his ship *The Clove* into the seas off the island of Hirado. He was entertained by the local daimyo, Matsuura Shigenobu, and made plans to visit the Shogun in Edo. While waiting in Hirado Saris celebrated the anniversary of the King's coronation by firing guns from his ship.

This appears to have entertained the locals, and Matsuura Shigenobu gave Saris a present of a suit of armour that he had worn during the Korean campaign. Sadly this historic armour has long since been lost.

Saris eventually made it to Edo and with the help of William Adams began negotiations with Hidetada over establishing trade rights. Both Hidetada and Adams were keen on the English venture being set up not far from Edo, but Saris insisted that the East India Company should copy the decision of its Dutch equivalent and establish itself on distant Hirado. It has long been a mystery why two international trading companies should choose a location so remote from the centre of government, although the most reasonable explanation is that its remoteness was seen as a positive asset.

Much of the Dutch trading activity was of questionable legality and included the interception of Portuguese shipping. So the English followed suit, and at the conclusion of the negotiations Hidetada presented Saris with gifts that included two armours. They had been made by Iwai Yosaemon, Tokugawa Ieyasu's own armourer. The suit shown here is a *nimai-dō*, in other words one that is made from two main sections opening with a long hinge under the left arm. It bears a *mon* that has been associated with the Takeda family. John Saris was only in Japan for three months so it is most unlikely that the armours were made to order, but the Shogun would no doubt have had many in his wardrobe!

To the contemporary English Japan was a remote and poorly understood country, as shown by the descriptions of the two armours that were made in inventories over the ensuing decades. In 1649 the objects are described as 'Indian' armours, while in 1660 they are noted as having been presented to the King by 'The Great Moghul'. Now fully restored to their original condition, these unique diplomatic gifts also bears the correct attribution of their origins.

64

The *kokka ankō* Bell of the Hōkōji

方広寺国家安康の鐘

Wars may be started for many different reasons and on many spurious pretexts. In 1614 a war broke out that was to lead to the destruction of Toyotomi Hideyori, Hideyoshi's heir and the only possible surviving challenger to the new dominance of the Tokugawa family. It was justified on the basis of an insulting description cast into the side of this temple bell.

Toyotomi Hideyori (1593-1615) was securely based within the protection of his late father's masterpiece of Osaka Castle. He had lived there since the defeat of his supporters at Sekigahara in 1600 and had been peacefully engaged for many years on the rebuilding of the Great Buddha of Kyōto.

As early as 1588 Hideyoshi had conceived the idea of creating a superlative religious image for the spiritual welfare of the nation. That Japan's spiritual wellbeing was not the sole consideration soon became apparent when Hideyoshi set in motion his notorious 'Sword Hunt'. This was a process by which offensive weapons of all kinds were forcibly removed from minor daimyō, temples, farmers, sea captains and anyone else of whom Hideyoshi did not approve. The official line was that the weapons were to be melted down and used to provide metal bolts for the construction of the Great Buddha, but it is likely that very few were used for this purpose. The Great Buddha was nevertheless constructed, only to be totally destroyed in the great earthquake of 1596.

The cynical Tokugawa Ieyasu believed that its replacement would be a fitting memorial to the great Hideyoshi and also an ideal way of bankrupting his heir. By 1602 the second image was complete up to the level of its neck, but as the workmen were engaged in casting the head early in 1603 the scaffolding caught fire and the entire statue was reduced to ashes along with the temple that housed it.

Work resumed in 1608 and in 1612 after a considerable expenditure a colossal statue of Buddha that rivalled those of Nara and Kamakura finally rose above the temple of Hōkōji in Japan's ancient capital. The only thing that remained to be done before the final dedication of the temple was the casting of a bell.

This was carried out but the inscription on it was found to bear the phrase *kokka ankō*, 'May the state be peaceful and prosperous'. *Ka* and *kō* were the Chinese-style readings of the characters read in the Japanese style as *ie* and *yasu*, so Tokugawa Ieyasu complained that in separating the two ideographs that made up his name, Hideyori was mocking him.

Elsewhere on the bell was another sentence that read 'On the East it welcomes the bright moon, on the West bids farewell to the setting sun'. This further aggrieved Ieyasu, who claimed that this alluded to him in Eastern Japan as the inferior and Hideyori the greater luminary, with a veiled threat that Hideyori intended

his destruction. It was a petty complaint, but it provided an excuse for Tokugawa Ieyasu to threaten Hideyori with force. By then it was September 1614, and reports soon reached Edo that Hideyori was inviting unemployed and dispossessed *rōnin* (lordless samurai) into Osaka castle to provide a strengthened garrison in the case of an attack. Within a very few months that expectation became reality.

65

Statue of Tomura Yoshikuni

戸村義国木像

Tomura Yoshikuni's life-like funerary effigy stands in the Ryōshō-In, the Tomura's family temple just below Yokote castle in Akita Prefecture. It commemorates his bravery in 1614; centuries later it would inspire a descendant to even greater feats of samurai glory.

Yoshikuni's action happened at Osaka where he fought for the Tokugawa against Toyotomi Hideyori and his *rōnin*. They, and the daimyō who had lost lands after Sekigahara, had seen an opportunity for revenge and a chance to regain what they had lost. Other daimyō who had been on the losing side took the opposite view and saw Osaka as an opportunity to regain the favour of the Tokugawa by defeating their enemies. One of those was Satake Yoshinobu (1570-1633), who was to fight eagerly for the Tokugawa at the battle of Imafuku in 1614, one of the crucial actions whereby the besieging Tokugawa army took control of the outlying positions around Osaka Castle. Tomura Yoshikuni was a Satake samurai.

At one stage during the battle the Satake were driven back by a suicidal charge. One samurai who was caught up in the melee was Yoshikuni, who was then aged twenty-four. He had climbed up on to the embankment along with his flag bearer and was met by a hail of enemy fire. Two arrows pierced his left arm and numerous arquebus bullets hit him in the side. As he fell in unbearable pain his retainer Nakayama Shichi'emon jumped down to help him.

Yoshikuni had been almost stunned by the fall, but he rose to his feet very unsteadily and tried to make his way again towards the enemy. Shichi'emon could see that he was delirious and almost lapsing into unconsciousness, and as his master fell again he took Yoshikuni by the shoulders and tried to drag him back towards the Satake lines. Yoshikuni was a heavily built man and unfortunately also kept a tight hold on to his spear, which proved to be a considerable additional hindrance. Even though Shichi'emon politely requested him to let go of the spear he would not abandon it, so with a supreme effort the slightly built Shichi'emon dragged him back as far as the edge of some impassable marshy ground. Just then a samurai appeared on a grey horse, lifted Yoshikuni on to his saddle and took him across the swamp to safety.

When Shichi'emon made his way back to the Satake headquarters with Yoshikuni he did not fail to tell the story of the anonymous samurai who had helped them, and because the mysterious man was never identified a legend grew within the Tomura family that he had been a personification of the Buddha. The following year Tomura Yoshikuni was summoned to Nijo Castle in Kyōto and received an official letter of commendation and a fine sword from the Shogun. His grandson would later be given responsibility for the castle of Yokote, a place that would see action 300 years later as will be related below, and once again a Tomura would show stubbornness in battle.

131

66

Ema of Sanada Yukimura

真田幸村の絵馬

Sanada Yukimura (1570-1615) was the finest general on the Toyotomi side at the siege of Osaka, and is shown here on an *ema* (prayer board) at the shrine that was built to console his unhappy spirit on the site of the place where he met his end. This ensured that he would not become an angry ghost.

Yukimura was killed during the second phase of the siege which is known as the Summer Campaign. Sanada Yukimura took the lead and an important decision was made. The Toyotomi side could not risk another siege of Osaka Castle. Instead they would engage the Tokugawa in battle.

The resulting battle of Tennōji in fields to the south of the castle began in dense fog and was very confusing to both sides. Sanada Yukimura, advancing at the head of his victorious samurai, saw Tokugawa Ieyasu virtually unprotected and engaged him in single combat. One version of the story has Ieyasu wounded by a spear thrust to his kidneys. The other, outrageous version, tells us that Tokugawa Ieyasu was killed and that his place on the battlefield was immediately taken by a *kagemusha* (double), so that his men would not lose heart. If anyone doubts this story, say the Toyotomi conspiracy theorists, then he

must visit the Nanshūji temple in Sakai, where Tokugawa Ieyasu is buried. His name is on the gravestone, just to prove it.

If Tokugawa Ieyasu had been killed in that encounter, and there is no evidence to suggest that he was, then it would have happened at about the same time that Sanada Yukimura (and without question it was the real Sanada Yukimura!) was also killed. This tragic event, which happened in the open and with many witnesses, occurred when Yukimura, too tired to fight on, collapsed exhausted on a camp stool. A Tokugawa samurai recognised him. Yukimura confirmed his identity and took off his helmet. The man lopped off Yukimura's head and rode off in triumph with the crucial trophy. Yukimura's remains were cremated and his spirit enshrined on the battlefield. Worshippers still write their petitions to him on these *ema* and hang them from a frame within the shrine grounds.

（新撰日本外史より）

133

The Hachisuka Navy

蜂須賀家の海軍

The symbol of the swastika rightly sends a shiver down the spine of most Europeans or Americans, and its not infrequent appearance in Japan, such as those shown here on a painted screen depicting the sails of the battle fleet maintained by the Hachisuka daimyō, provokes many questions among visitors who encounter it.

They need not worry. The *manji* symbol, as it is known in Japanese, has its origins in ancient Buddhist belief as a symbol of eternity or 'myriad things'. The homonym of *man* means 10,000, and any map of Japan will have Buddhist temples marked with the sign of the *manji*.

The Hachisuka family first came to prominence under Hachisuka Masakatsu (1525-1585), and a colourful legend relates how Masakatsu first met his future master Toyotomi Hideyoshi. Masakatsu was at that time the leader of a gang of thieves and encountered the young Hideyoshi during one of his nightly forays. He was impressed by the boy who dared to answer him back after being kicked by the robbers, so he invited Hideyoshi to join in their burglary.

Many years later the Hachisuka would become prominent daimyō just like Hideyoshi, having risen from obscurity in the way for which the unruly Sengoku Period provided many opportunities. Hachisuka Iemasa (1558-1638) succeeded his father and took part in Hideyoshi's invasion of Shikoku in 1585. He acquired lands on Shikoku as a reward, and his descendants were to occupy the Tokushima area for many centuries as daimyō.

Fortunately for the family Hachisuka Yoshishige (1581-1615), whose fleet is shown here, chose the winning side at Sekigahara and was confirmed in his lands as a result. Contemporary painted screens of these battles show the Hachisuka contingent clearly defined by the *manji* on their flags.

Another daimyō to use the *manji* symbol was Tsugaru Nobuhira (1586-1631), whose *shakujō* battle standard was noted earlier. This simple *jingasa* (helmet) worn by his foot soldiers bears a *manji*, as would the breastplates of their armour and the samurai's *sashimono* flags.

Surcoat and Armour for a daimyo

陣羽織と大名具足

A claim that a certain suit of armour was once owned by a famous individual is frequently made but often difficult to prove.

Armours were commissioned and many were presented as gifts, and often their sole purpose was to adorn a daimyō's private chamber where he could sit beside this striking symbol of his martial greatness. A specially commissioned armour would reflect the daimyō's personal tastes, hence the tall helmets seen earlier that were owned by the Maeda family. In general, armours made only for show would tend to be far more elaborate in their choice of fittings and decoration than ones made for battlefield use, and for obvious reasons fewer armours made for use in war have survived. This modest example may well fall into the latter category. It is of a straightforward design and is associated with Sakakibara Yasumasa.

Sakakibara Yasumasa (1548-1600) served Tokugawa Ieyasu as one of the *shi-ten*, his four most faithful samurai, a title that is derived from the expression for the four guardian kings of heaven in Japanese religious belief. He fought at the battles of Anegawa, Mikatagahara and Nagashino, to name but a few.

The armour shown here is a *nimai-dō* laced in *kebiki* style, the traditional form of numerous lamellae bound together. The *kusazuri* (skirt pieces), the *shikoro* (helmet neck guard) and the face mask are all finished with a bottom layer of black bear's fur. The gold ornamentation suggests a samurai of some financial means, but the association with Sakakibara Yasumasa comes from the choice of *mon* used here and there to decorate the armour. It is the Buddhist wheel of the law, a design found on other suits that Yasumasa owned. Its inclusion reflects his commitment to Buddhism, and a suit of armour of his owned by Tokyo National Museum which also has the same *mon* includes a helmet that bears as its *maedate* (front crest) the two edged sword that is associated with Buddhism and often appears in the hands of the god Fudō Myo-ō.

One can therefore easily imagine Sakakibara Yasumasa directing his troops while wearing this armour, and it is more than likely that he would also have been wearing a *jinbaori*, the ornamental surcoat worn by high-ranking samurai. These were normally sleeveless, and the unbroken expanse of the rear of a *jinbaori* provided a canvas for some very imaginative designs. This example from Akita bears the *mon* of a white crane that was used by several families.

Shōki, The Queller of Demons

宝泉院の血天井

In Chinese mythology his name is Zhong Kui; in Japanese he is Shōki. In both cultures he is the queller of demons.

Clad in a black costume associated with his origins in Tang China, this fierce entity is a more than appropriate subject to paint upon a samurai's war banner such as this example where he appears on the flag of a retainer of the Satake daimyō of Akita.

The mythology surrounding Shōki tells a sad tale. He is said to have been a physician in the province of Shensi but was very ugly. To advance his career prospects he took the examination which would result in imperial service and scored the top mark. But when Zhong Kui was presented to Emperor Xuanzong he was rejected on account of his looks and committed suicide in remorse. The emperor was grief stricken, but once when he fell ill Zhong Kui appeared to him in a dream and subdued the demons causing his sickness. In gratitude the emperor posthumously awarded Zhong Kui the title he had coveted, and from then on the queller of demons acted in a protective capacity. The image on the banner shows Shōki in an unusual pose, because he is generally shown with one of the demons he has caught (or failed to catch). Sometimes they are shown playing tricks on him to avoid capture. Otherwise he holds his wriggling victim by the scruff of the neck.

Shōki appeared on one of the large banners carried into battle by the father and son team of Maeda Toshiie and Toshinaga. Maeda Toshiie also owned a *jinbaori* with a picture of Shōki on the back. The smaller picture shows an additional manifestation of Shōki in Japanese culture. This gigantic straw figure armed with bow and sword is called Shōki-sama and has been made by the local villagers in Niigata Prefecture to protect their homes and fields against evil in the coming year.

Armour of yukinoshita-dō Style

雪の下胴

The development of firearms posed a severe challenge to Japanese armour makers. The hole in the foot soldier's **okegawa-dō** shown earlier demonstrated what bullets could do, and by the beginning of the seventeenth century styles of armour were being introduced that were claimed to be bullet-proof. In some cases, they were sold with dents from test firing to reassure the customer.

Most designs involved some form of solid plate *dō* (body armour) in place of ones made in the traditional way from numerous small scales. A *namban-dō*, a Spanish soldier's armour converted to Japanese tastes, was one answer. Japanese manufactured armours made use of a handful of solid plates riveted together, and if the separate sections were fastened horizontally the armour was called a *yokohagi-dō*. *Tatehagi-dō* was the name given to one made from vertical plates. It might be lacquered all over to eliminate the joins (*hotoke-dō*) or left bare like this fine example. Its surface is of russet iron produced by controlled rust and then lacquered. This particular style of body armour was made by Myōchin Hisaie and was known by the name of his home town as a *yukinoshita-dō*.

Yukinoshita-dō armours were the favourite of the great daimyō Date Masamune (1566-1636) of Sendai. He equipped all his troops in these solid bullet-proof armours, giving them the name of *sendai-dō* after his castle town.

A bust of Masamune appears in the smaller picture wearing a *yukinoshita-dō* along with an equally strong helmet adorned with

an elaborate crescent moon *maedate*. In 1600 Date Masamune acted on Tokugawa Ieyasu's behalf to subdue the supporters of Ishida Mitsunari in Tōhoku. He defeated Ieyasu's deadliest enemy in the north, Uesugi Kagekatsu and received as a reward twelve districts that the Uesugi had owned. He died at the age of seventy, renowned as a warrior and a diplomat.

Ema of Yamada Nagamasa

山田長政の絵馬

The most famous Japanese ever to serve in Siam was Yamada Nagamasa (1578-1633), whose life has been much embellished by romantic legend and propaganda. He began his career as a merchant trading with Siam, hence this votive ema (prayer board) depicting Nagamasa in his ship. This larger style of ema is a variation of the small prayer boards as depicted in Object 66. They were normally about two metres in area and were hung on the walls of temples. The original (of which this is modern copy) was presented to a temple in Shizuoka, Nagamasa's birthplace.

When in Siam Yamada Nagamasa turned his attentions and abilities to matters that went far beyond trade. He and his fellow Japanese were closely involved in the events that brought about the succession of King Song Tham between 1611 and 1628 and went on to serve him.

Nagamasa became the king's closest advisor in the royal palace of Ayutthaya where loyal Japanese samurai acted as the King's bodyguard. When King Song Tham died his vacant throne was contested by a usurper with the title of the Kalahom, the minister of military affairs, whose rise to power was challenged most forcefully by the Japanese in royal service. In 1629 the Kalahom first ensured that Yamada Nagamasa was out of the way by sending him to quell a rebellion in Ligor (modern Nakhon Si Thammarat). He then ordered the expulsion of the Japanese from Ayutthaya.

The plot came to the ears of the Japanese, who took the initiative and fought back.

There was some bloodshed before they agreed to leave peacefully for Ligor, but the Ayutthaya affair was by no means over. Eight samurai had been absent on a pilgrimage to a Buddhist temple, and when they returned to the capital they were arrested and put in jail. They did not stay there for long, because news arrived that Siam was in peril from a pirate raid.

The captives were promised their liberty if they would help rid the country of the invaders. They proposed that as many Siamese troops as possible should be equipped with Japanese armour and helmets, the sight of which would terrify the attackers. Eight war elephants were also made available. The samurai took command of the disguised company together with an additional 500 Siamese soldiers, and placed a couple of small cannon on the back of each elephant. As they came in sight of the raiding ships they began a furious cannonade which would have sunk the whole fleet had they not prudently retreated.

It was the most unusual victory secured by Japanese in royal service and added greatly to the Yamada Nagamasa legend.

143

Secret Christian Tea Bowl

潜伏キリシタンの茶碗

This object symbolises two contrasting and sometimes conflicting elements in the religious history of Japan. It is a tea bowl for use during the tea ceremony, the Zen-inspired ritual beloved of so many samurai. But it also bears upon it a stylised Christian cross. Is this evidence that its owner was a secret Christian?

By the 1620s the position of Christianity in Japan had changed radically from the situation of tolerance that had characterised the time of Bernardo Nagasaki and his Jesuit allies. Oda Nobunaga had been sympathetic to Christianity, but Toyotomi Hideyoshi saw parallels between the Christian daimyō and the Buddhist fanatics whom he had spent so many years fighting. The possibility of an invasion of Japan by Spain, assisted by a fifth column of Christian samurai, may have been highly unlikely, but it was enough for Hideyoshi to regard it as a challenge to his authority.

In 1597 twenty-six prominent Christians were martyred in Nagasaki. Persecution intensified under the Tokugawa until the only priests active in Japan were ones who had been smuggled in by Portuguese and Spanish traders. Yet instead of wiping out the faith completely the church went underground. That was the beginning of the epic story of the secret Christians.

It is an interesting comment on samurai society that members of the samurai class were the first to abandon the faith when

persecution threatened. Some loyal believers like Naitō Yukiyasu were exiled to Manila. A few were killed, but many returned to the religious beliefs of their ancestors. That a samurai skilled in the tea ceremony, the quintessence of Japanese culture, could also have been a secret Christian would have been an almost unique instance. Instead the maintenance and dissemination of Christian beliefs fell on to the shoulders of the lower classes.

They kept the faith going in spite of the attempts made to locate the secret believers over the ensuing decades. One method was to assemble all the inhabitants of a village once a year and make them tread on a holy picture or medallion obtained by the authorities from a previous raid. Any reluctance to do this would immediately arouse suspicion. Imprisonment and torture would follow, but the victim's death was not usually the goal of the interrogators. Instead they preferred the prisoner to make a public recantation of his religion, an act that would discourage others. The communities who survived lived in fear but were sustained by faith.

Grave of Matsukura Shigemasa

松倉重政の墓

A reclining Buddha, an unusual style for Japan where seated or standing figures are the norm, lies next to the grave of Matsukura Shigemasa in Shimabara (Nagasaki Prefecture). It is a powerful Buddhist image and a very appropriate statue to be placed next to the last resting place of a man who was one of the greatest enemies of Christianity that Japan ever had. He was also the daimyō who suggested the most radical way of solving the Christian problem.

Matsukura Shigemasa (1574-1630) was the daimyō of Shimabara, and many of his subjects were the children or grandchildren of people who had embraced Christianity when the Portuguese Jesuits moved freely among them. They were to suffer greatly at Shigemasa's hands, but Shigemasa's tyranny was by no means confined to the followers of one particular religion. His favourite trick – that of tying victims inside a straw raincoat, setting it on fire and watching them 'dance' – became notorious. He also used the natural boiling volcanic waters of Unzen as a torture to make suspect Christians confess their faith and recant. Then, when cruelty and persecution appeared not to work, Matsukura turned his attentions to the supply side of the Christian problem.

In spite of a ban on pain of death, foreign priests were still slipping into Japan and ministering secretly to the people. Consequently, in 1630 Shigemasa proposed a bold move to the Shogun's councillors. The main source of supply for foreign priests was Manila, the capital of the Spanish possession of the Philippines. Taking his cue from the successful annexation of the Ryūkyūs by the Shimazu, he requested permission to lead an invasion of the Philippines. So confident

was he that his desire would be granted that he sent two retainers to Manila disguised as merchants to spy out the defences. They were hardly ninja (!) because the Spanish guessed immediately what their mission was, but before he could

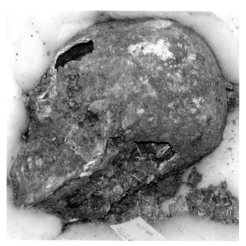

receive the go-ahead Matsukura Shigemasa died.

The idea of an invasion of the Philippines was reawakened in 1637. The scheme now had additional support in the shape of the Dutch, whose anti-Catholic prejudices led them to offer the Japanese ships and equipment for the invasion of a colony of their hated Spanish enemies. The decision

to go ahead was made at the end of the year. Ten thousand troops were earmarked for the expedition, but at that point the situation in Shimabara changed dramatically.

Shigemasa's heir Shigeharu had been as bad a tyrant as his late father, and while the invasion army was being mustered a rebellion broke out in Matsukura territory. Although it had a considerable Christian tinge the Shimabara Rebellion of 1637-38 was a massive uprising by the oppressed lower classes in general. Their early successes first stunned the Tokugawa Shogunate and then embarrassed it by taking over a year to quell. The smaller picture shows the remains of one of the Christian victims who died in the final challenge to Tokugawa rule that Japan would ever see.

148

74

'Strange Helmets'

変わり兜

The solid and practical-looking battle dress armours of the Sengoku Period were made to be worn in action. Ornamentation was kept to a minimum to allow the maximum freedom of movement compatible with the wearer's protection.

The box-like *yoroi* was now rarely seen except for ceremonial wear, and samurai armour generally presented a uniformity of appearance, making an army look like a swarm of identical black beetles. In spite of these practical requirements, or maybe even because of them, a certain individuality of style is evident on many surviving examples of helmet. The tall specimens favoured by the Maeda family were noted earlier, but evidence from contemporary painted screens suggests the helmet provided the opportunity for a samurai of even modest means to stand out from the crowd.

The result was a rich mixture of military headgear known simply as *kawari kabuto* (strange helmets). Sea shells, antlers, courtiers' caps and buffalo horns could be built up on top of the basic protective helmet using wood or papier-mache. Katō Kiyomasa of Kumamoto had his favourite *naga eboshi no kabuto* (long courtier's cap helmet), built up on top of a simple bowl.

The helmet shown here is a glorious joke. Its bowl is made like a *jingasa*, the simple helmets issued to the foot soldiers, but in the style worn by samurai on official duties in Edo. It has been fitted with a *shikoro*, the lacing of which is protected from the elements by a leather cover. Its most striking feature is of course the golden *maedate*, a frontal crest of a hare with large ears. Is it perhaps a rich samurai's way of proclaiming the he was better than others?

The Art of Swimming in Armour

水術

The martial arts of archery, swordsmanship and hand-to-hand combat are well known, but the samurai had to be ready for anything. On many occasions he would be required to cross water in some way or another so the ability to swim was vital.

Tokugawa Ieyasu encouraged swimming and regularly swam in the moat of Edo Castle. There are several stories in Japanese history of samurai who swam their horses across rivers in order to be the first into a battle, and various forms of float were developed to allow a samurai to swim while wearing his suit of armour.

Various schools of martial arts developed that specialised in swimming under water or swimming in rapids. The former was demonstrated in no uncertain fashion during the siege of Ota Castle in 1585. Toyotomi Hideyoshi built a dyke and diverted a river to make a huge lake that allowed his warships to sail in from the estuary and bombard the castle from close range. The commander of the garrison responded by sending divers who swam underneath the hulls of the ships and bored holes into them to make them sink.

Other schools specialised in grappling techniques in water. The Hosokawa daimyō, who took over Kumamoto Castle from Katō Kiyomasa, went much further and developed a school of martial arts called the Kobori-ryū that was dedicated to swimming techniques including the use of weapons while treading water. A samurai trained in Kobori-ryū *suijutsu* (swimming techniques) could operate a bow and arrow while suspended by his floats. The illustration shows the technique that must have been the most difficult of all: to fire an arquebus while treading water without the lighted fuse becoming soaked, while the photograph from Kumamoto Castle confirms that the techniques of swimming in armour are still performed to this day.

Ainu Ear Mound

アイヌ耳塚

Japan's northern island of Hokkaidō, then called Ezo, was Tokugawa Japan's final frontier. On Hokkaidō lived tribes collectively known as the Ainu and clashes developed with the Shogun's forces as Japanese colonisation proceeded.

Only one daimyō held lands on Hokkaidō; this was the Matsumae family to whom the Shogun had granted a monopoly on trade in 1644, and in the grounds of their castle stands this mound that contains the ears taken from the heads of fourteen Ainu tribesmen who opposed them in 1669. The smaller picture shows Ainu captives.

There had been armed conflict with the Ainu as early as 1456, but the war that was to end so tragically for the Ainu began as a fight for resources between two confederations of their own tribes led by Onibishi and Shakushain.

In 1668 Shakushain, a warrior in his eighties, led an attack upon Onibishi and his men who were holed up inside a Japanese mining camp. The camp was burned to the ground, so the incident was inevitably seen in Edo as an act of aggression against the Japanese colonists. Responding in kind, Shakushain took over a wider coalition of tribes and began attacking other mining camps together with the Matsumae's trading posts and even visiting Japanese ships.

The Matsumae daimyō appears to have been taken completely by surprise by the ferocity of the rebellion that led to 270 Japanese deaths, and asked for outside help. Shakushain then advanced upon Matsumae's castle but was met by a force of eighty Japanese armed with muskets. The Ainu retreated, only to be pursued by reinforcements until Shakushain surrendered. It appeared that a peaceful settlement had been reached, but at a drinking party to celebrate the end of hostilities Shakushain was murdered along with three of his generals. His fortress was then burned down.

Why had it been felt necessary to murder Shakushain? The answer probably lies with the position Japan had chosen for itself in the world. The Sakoku Edict of 1639 had closed Japan off from contact with Europe and the Christian threat of invasion from Spain. The Manchu takeover of China in 1644 had then showed that Japan might be vulnerable to similar pressure from the north, so Hokkaidō and the Ainu had to be pacified. This almost anonymous mound is the memorial to that belief.

77

Mansenshūkai and the Water Spider

萬川集海と水蜘蛛

No book about samurai would be complete without some mention of ninja, the black-clad assassins and spies whose superlative martial skills delivered in an underhand way turned the samurai tradition on its head.

That popular view, illustrated by this life-sized plastic ninja at the Toei Film Studios theme park in Kyoto, however, is a modern exaggeration of something that existed in a very different form when samurai had wars to fight. One of the most important ways in which historical fact was translated into martial myth came about through the production of the so-called 'ninja manuals' during the time of peace. This is an illustration from the most famous of them, *Mansenshūkai*, compiled in 1676, and the picture chosen is of probably the most misunderstood item of 'ninja equipment', the *mizugumo*, the wooden 'water spider' that is popularly believed to allow a ninja to walk on water.

There are many well-recorded instances of spying, assassination and undercover warfare within Japanese history. It would be surprising if there had been none, because Japan was no different from any other military society in making use of covert activities, but none was carried out by ninja as the term is usually understood. The name itself would alone have baffled any Sengoku Period daimyō, as it is a modern reading of a two character compound *shinobi no mono* that means a practitioner of secrecy. The expression implies a dedicated cult-like art passed on only to the initiated, and that is indeed how the term is popularly understood. A *shinobi no mono* is regarded as belonging to an elite school or tradition

dedicated to *ninjutsu*, the arts of secrecy, and having no personal allegiance other than to himself, he hired his services out on a mercenary basis to other daimyō.

The historical evidence, however, points to a very different conclusion, because when the character *shinobi* is used in descriptions of such activities it is employed as an adverb, not a noun. It indicates how something was done rather than who did it. It is most frequently encountered in the phrase *shinobi itte* 'entered in secret' with reference to an attack on a castle, but it can have a far more mundane meaning because secret movement can also be in a reverse direction, as in the *Shinchō-Kō ki* reference to the cowardly Araki Muneshige, 'On the night of the 2nd day of the Ninth Month, Araki Settsu no kami slipped out (*shinobi dete*) of Itami Castle'.

In the Iga-Ueno Ninja Museum their copy of *Mansenshūkai* is labelled the 'ninja bible', but why should its author have chosen to reveal so many secrets? He gives us an answer at the end of his introduction. It is 'to preserve the secrets of these military matters before they are lost forever'. To someone dwelling in the mid-seventeenth century the time had passed when any of these devices or techniques could be of any use. He wished to preserve the knowledge before it was lost forever.

As for the 'water spider', it has long been regarded as a pair of huge water shoes, and several ninja museums show its use in that way. In fact it is a simple flotation device, and the user would actually sit on the middle section.

155

78

Hanging Scroll of the Matsuura Army

松浦軍団掛物

This large *kakemono* displayed in the Matsuura Historical Museum in Hirado shows the Matsuura army prepared for battle, even though no engagement then took place. The picture is in fact an ideal arrangement of troops in 1796 as set out by the great strategist Yamaga Soko (1622-1685).

The 29th daimyō of Hirado, Matsuura Shigenobu (1637-1689) was on intimate terms with Soko and organised the Matsuura army according to Yamaga's recommendations. A century later the enthusiastic 34th daimyō Matsuura Seizan Kiyoshi (1775-1806) followed his predecessor's lead by outfitting and training his troops in the Yamaga mode, and it is more than likely that he would have actually paraded his troops in this way.

Taking the layout as a whole, Soko's ideas with regard to battle formations were nothing revolutionary, and the positions adopted by Matsuura Kiyoshi are very similar to several standard battle formations recommended by military thinkers during the Sengoku Period. Spearmen protect arquebusiers to front, flanks and rear, and the samurai form a third rank, while the general is surrounded by a half-circle of retainers, with flags and drum to hand. The scroll shows 650 men of whom 238 may be identified as support troops. This figure (37% of the total) is reached after including within the fighting men all the flag bearers and drummers.

Matsuura Seizan Kiyoshi is shown on the scroll wearing a green-laced armour with a helmet covered in white polar-bear fur. This is on display in Hirado castle. His attendants include bodyguard samurai, spearmen, weapon-bearers, baggage carriers, cup bearers and grooms, as befits his rank. The samurai who wear individual suits of armour and a *sashimono* (back flag) of red and white would appear to be the senior ranks among Kiyoshi's immediate bodyguard, and are placed very close to him. The *ashigaru* spearmen wear red armour with diagonal gold stripes. A semi-circle of samurai in two different uniform designs of black and red armour completes his bodyguard. A specimen of the striped armour is also on show in Hirado castle. None of the above samurai appear to have personal attendants, but the mounted samurai are each attended by between six and eight men, one of whom is a groom. The foot samurai who form the third fighting rank also have a personal attendant each who carries his polearm. The specialised *ashigaru* units number off as arquebuses 104 (58%), archers 32 (18%) and spearmen 42 (24%). They are grouped in fours or fives, with three or four gunners and one archer in each group, and an officer in attendance. There are ten groups in the front and ten in the rear ranks. Behind them are the rows of spearmen, the blades of their weapons concealed within ornate scabbards.

The Matsuura *kakemono* thus provides unique historical evidence for the appearance of the army of a daimyō during the long peace of the Tokugawa Period. Its balance of troops, its careful layout, and the link between rank and income thus produced the final flowering of the samurai army.

79

Ōishi Yoshio's Baton of Command

大石良雄の采配

Many great Japanese battles were started by the lowering of a commander's *saihai* (war fan or baton of command), but none can have launched a more memorable assault than the one shown here.

This *saihai* belonged to Ōishi Yoshio, the leader of the Loyal Retainers of Akō, popularly known as the Forty-Seven Rōnin. It is customary to regard the Raid of the Forty-Seven Rōnin in 1703 as the classic act of revenge, the supreme *katakiuchi* (vendetta) of Old Japan, yet an examination of the incident shows that the famous night raid stretched the definition of a vendetta to breaking point. *Katakiuchi* had the literal reading of 'cutting down an enemy' and meant that someone, either the victim or his close representative, would take immediate revenge on a killer. The Forty-Seven Rōnin, by contrast, took delayed revenge on a victim.

Their victim was the 60-year-old Kira Yoshihisa. By 1701 he had served successive Shoguns as a loyal and utterly reliable master of court ceremonial for about forty years. It was a role that required minute attention to detail and clockwork precision. A man in that position, one can safely assume, did not suffer fools gladly, and when faced with having to instruct in etiquette the young Asano Naganori, daimyō of Akō to whom court ceremonial was much less interesting than court ladies, Yoshihisa's self-control was to be tested to the limit.

Yet it was not Lord Kira who exploded in anger inside Edo Castle. It was his pupil, and Asano attacked Kira with a sword. Even

to draw a weapon inside Edo Castle was a very serious offence, but Asano received very rough justice. The order for his execution was delivered at 4 pm that same day and he committed *seppuku* two hours later. The speed of the process meant that the motive for Asano's act would never be known, but with their master dead and hugely disgraced his former retainers faced the prospect of becoming unemployed *rōnin*. They therefore resolved to kill Kira and place his head upon Asano's tomb. The fact that Asano's death had been ordered

by the Shogun rather than Kira was conveniently ignored. Put quite simply, their lord had failed to kill Kira. They would finish the job in his memory.

All the legends and plays based on the event tell us that the Forty-Seven Rōnin attempted to put Kira off his guard by living lives that suggested to the outside world that they had abandoned any ideas of revenge or of ever becoming respectable samurai again. So the famous surprise raid took place, and in the process of achieving their supposedly honourable objective the Forty-Seven Rōnin slaughtered seventeen of Lord Kira's own samurai, who died bravely and innocently in his defence. In military terms the Forty-Seven Rōnin achieved their objective: to take the head of Kira Yoshihisa and place it before the tomb of Asano Naganori.

They then surrendered themselves to the authorities and committed *seppuku* en masse, thus becoming the great heroes of samurai behaviour. Lord Kira and his men were sent to their almost unknown graves; the Forty-Seven Rōnin were sent to glory.

80

Fire Helmet

火事兜

Violent incidents such as the Raid of the Forty-Seven Rōnin were mercifully rare during the Edo Period. Usually the most challenging and dangerous task that a samurai could be called upon to perform was to act as a fireman.

The samurai firemen were called *hatamoto-hikeshi*, with higher-ranking ones known as *daimyō-hikeshi*. To be appointed as a *daimyō-hikeshi* was a great honour. There were also civilian fire brigades (*machi-hikeshi*) recruited from among the townspeople whose members sported tattoos. A dragon, with its association was water, was a favourite because it was believed to repel fire. The daimyō's brigades wore helmets such as the one shown here.

It resembles a normal samurai helmet except that instead of the multi-plate *shikoro* there is a long cloak that ties round the face. This one is of red Dutch cloth and bears the *mon* of the Mōri family. The fire officer would also wear *hakama* (trousers) and his sword would be thrust through a flame-resistant belt as he gave orders for a fire to be controlled. During the 1760s hand operated water pumps were introduced. Otherwise a bucket chain from the Sumida River or cutting firebreaks, which the *daimyō-hikeshi* undertook with gusto, was the most effective means of controlling a blaze.

Fire prevention was also a very serious business for a samurai firemen. So many

people lived in the capital that their wooden houses were packed tightly together. The daimyō mansions (*yashiki*) were extensive structures of barracks and reception halls, and if a daimyō allowed a fire to start inside his *yashiki* he would be punished, although the penalty was usually withdrawn if the fire did not spread. Some *yashiki* were fitted with a lookout tower called a *hinomi*. Mounted on it was a bell and a striking board. Their sounds were often heard, because during the 250 years of the Edo Period there were twenty large fires and three large earthquakes in the capital.

In the great fire of 1657 half of the city of Edo was destroyed and over 100,000 people lost their lives, but on one occasion towards the end of the Edo Period the rivalry between the daimyō and town firemen almost caused a disaster of its own. The *machi-hikeshi* under the charismatic Shinmon no Tatsugorō arrived at the scene of a fire to find the standard bearer of the Arima daimyō standing guard. Tempers frayed, and the two groups of firemen attacked each other with swords and fire axes. By the time order was restored eighteen men lay dead.

81

Sword Guards

鍔

The sword may have been the soul of the samurai, but as the peaceful Edo Period wore on and the sword became less of a weapon and more a badge of rank. The decorative aspect of a fine sword came to the fore.

Nowhere was this better illustrated than in the care and craftsmanship that went into producing sword fittings, and the sword guard or *tsuba* was a prime area for applying an artistic element to the sword's overall appearance. Its small surface area and individual shape provided an exciting challenge to craftsmen who worked in metal, and the *tsuba* shown here from Maruoka Castle in Fukui Prefecture were primarily decorative items where there had never been any intention of mounting them on to actual blades.

The majority of *tsuba* were worked in a soft homogenous iron that was free from flaws. Some would have attractive patinas added that yielded a range of tones from russet brown to deep blue black. Decorative features were produced using copper and its alloys such as *shakudo* (copper and

bronze) and *shibuichi* (copper and silver). Gold ensured particularly pleasing effects.

From left to right and from top to bottom the first has gilt designs of square spiral patterns. The copper inclusion within the hole for the tang of the sword indicates that this *tsuba* was made for use.

The second is of circular shape and shows clearly the three holes for the tang and the two utility knives. The six decorations are based on famous *mon* (family badges). The third *tsuba* has a design of cranes flying above golden grass, while its overall shape is made distinctive by hammering each corner into a folded-over curve. The final *tsuba* is the largest of the four. It shows four bearded sages being watched by an observer underneath a canopy of bamboo that disappears into the clouds.

82

A Conch Shell Trumpet

法螺貝

During a samurai battle the mournful tone of a _horagai_ like this could frequently be heard above the sound of an army's drums. A _horagai_ was a trumpet made from a conch shell fitted with a metal mouthpiece and with decorative carrying cords.

The _horagai_ are particularly associated with the _yamabushi_, the devotees of the religious sect of Shugendō, whose main means of religious expression was to undertake gruelling spiritual pilgrimages in mountains. A skilled _yamabushi_ could make a _horagai_ heard over a considerable distance, and the Hōjō family recruited _yamabushi_ as their trumpeters.

When a conch was blown the notes were not stopped or cut short; they began quietly and were raised in pitch to end with a high note, and there were various set sequences of _horagai_ calls that would be known to a particular army.

One source tells of a sequence of three conch signals for making ready for departure. On the first call eating must be abandoned or not begun. On the second the soldier must get himself ready, and on the third depart, with the vanguard taking the lead and the other units following. On actual departure the call was one single blow, then five sets of five blows, three sets of three blows, seven sets of seven blows, five sets of five blows, three sets of three blows and one single final blow, a pattern which followed the rhythm of a Buddhist chant. For advancing one's army by night, the call was seven conch blows, to which the reply of ten conch blows was given in confirmation.

In order to make it known to one's allies that a night attack was taking place the call was eight sets of eight conch blows, the number eight representing Hachiman, the god of war. The call to be given when it became apparent that the enemy was showing signs of being defeated was four sets of four conch blows, then four blows, then two sets of six blows, then four blows.

On this occasion the conch blowing also set the pace of the advance along with the drums. The conch call to order the extermination of an enemy was seven sets of seven conch blows, then five sets of five conch blows and three sets of three conch blows.

83

Helmets with Antlers

鹿角兜

The Vikings, as any schoolboy knows, did not wear horns on their helmets. The samurai did, as the pictures of 'strange helmets' earlier will have demonstrated, and two famous samurai owned helmets that sported wooden water buffalo horns.

Kuroda Nagamasa's helmet had huge golden horns, while Tokugawa Ieyasu had a suit of armour made from hide still covered in hair, with suitable horns to match. A deer's antlers could be an impressive variation, proclaiming on a battlefield the samurai's resemblance to a magnificent stag. Fukuchiyama Castle owns the helmet with golden antlers shown in the main picture. There is no attribution of ownership in this case, but similar golden antlers appeared on a helmet known to have been owned by Sakai Tadatsugu, one of Tokugawa Ieyasu's *shi-ten* and the man who beat the drum at Hamamatsu. Tadatsugu's helmet was lacquered red and resembles another antlered helmet associated with Sanada Yukimura of Osaka fame.

Honda Tadakatsu (1548-1610) is the fourth of Ieyasu's *shi-ten* to be mentioned in this book along with Sakai, Sakakibara and Ii. He served Ieyasu is all his campaigns. Tadakatsu was well known for wearing a helmet ornamented with stylised wooden antlers and was depicted in this guise on the contemporary painted screen of the battle of Nagashino.

The statue shown here is on the site of his castle of Kuwana to which he was transferred after the battle of Sekigahara with a much increased stipend. The effigy captures very well his armour, helmet and the large wooden Buddhist prayers beads that he customarily wore around his neck.

Helmet in the Style of a Human Head

総髪形兜

The splendid example of a 'strange helmet' shown here was known as a *sōgōnari kabuto*, or 'totally hairy helmet', whereby a very practical and efficient headpiece has been transformed using horse hair into a human scalp.

The helmet peak now represents the shaven part of the head above the forehead that was fashionable at the time, while the hair is drawn back and tied into a *motodori* (pigtail). A similar helmet owned by Tokyo National Museum is part of an even more fantastic ensemble because it is accompanied by a body section designed to represent the human torso. The inspiration for it was the emaciated shape of an elderly Buddhist monk, which is brought out in the contours of the chest and back. The monk's robe covers half his chest.

The other way in which the human body could be represented through armour was by developing the idea of a face mask. The first face masks were no more than a secure iron plate shaped to the contours of the chin that would allow the helmet cords to be tied more securely than they could be against bare flesh. In time the lower face mask was combined with the brow guard (often a feature of foot soldiers' equipment) to produce a defence for the whole face. It took little imagination to give it flaring

nostrils, a furrowed brow and even a moustache. There would also be a little hole to allow the perspiration to flow out. This specimen in Matsue Castle even has eyebrows.

Horse Armour

馬鎧

Throughout history the possession of a horse acted as a badge of rank for the wealthier members of the samurai class.

As we noted in the remarks concerning 'the way of bow and horse', skills at mounted archery once effectively defined what a samurai was. The archer of the Gempei War was well protected by his heavy *yoroi* armour, but the same could not be said for his unfortunate horse, because a few decorative tassels around its neck and rump were all the defences it had.

Horse armour was certainly known about at this time, but it is not until the late Sengoku Period that anything like a true suit of armour for a horse (*uma yoroi*) makes its appearance.

The one shown here is quite simple. It is made from lacquered leather scales. Note the typical heavy iron *abumi* (stirrups) and the large protective leather aprons that hung down from the saddle. Most horse armours were of three parts for the tail, the hindquarters and the neck.

This horse has some extra protection for its neck, but its *uma yoroi* is lacking in any defence for the face. Known as a chamfron in Europe and as a *bamen* (horse mask) in Japan these often took the form of a caricature of a horse's head or even a dragon. They were usually made from boiled and moulded leather and lacquered gold, red and black. Holes were left for the horse's eyes, but with the addition of horns, teeth and even fire coming out of its nostrils, a samurai's horse's could be converted into a comical monster. Toyotomi Hideyoshi owned the most gorgeous horse armour of all. The leather scales were lacquered gold and the black *bamen* resembled the head of a bull rather than a horse.

86

The Training Pole of the Jigen-ryū

示現流立木打ち

During the time of peace brought about by the triumph of the Tokugawa, the martial arts could flourish unhampered by any need to win battles. .

Some former samurai turned to the brush to deck the art of sword fighting with Zen philosophy; others set up schools of swordsmanship. One of the longest lasting schools still in existence today is the Jigen-ryū of Satsuma province, the seat of the Shimazu family of Satsuma. It was founded by a Satsuma samurai called Tōgō Shigekata, who had trained from the age of seven. At the age of thirteen this sword prodigy had used a dagger to quell a brawl, and at the age of eighteen he engaged in his first battle.

In 1588 the retired daimyō Shimazu Yoshihisa (1533-1611) went up to Kyōto to display his new loyalty to Hideyoshi. Tōgō Shigekata was ordered to go along with him as his attendant, and made the acquaintance of the Sōtō Zen priest Zenkitsu (1567-94), who was a sword master of the Jigen-ryū ('the school of self-discovery'), which emphasised the need for Zen meditation as part of the package of skills for a swordsman. This meeting, symbolised on the scroll in the second picture, added an entirely new dimension to Shigekata's appreciation of the art of sword fighting and he flourished as a pupil under Zenkitsu.

The enthusiastic Shigekata was eager to prove the worth of his newly acquired teaching and yearned to return to Satsuma and his old *sensei*. This finally happened in 1601.

Three years of hard practice and study followed Shigekata's return. The most important element of his physical regime was his own unique version of *suburi*, a practice technique akin to 'shadow-boxing'. The Jigen-ryū version consisted of repeatedly striking a wooden sword against a vertical wooden post. It is still practised within the modern Jigen-ryū to this day. The post, usually made from oak or chestnut wood, stands about two metres above the floor.

The swordsman, armed with a crude version of a *bokutō* (wooden practice sword) assumes the school's characteristic fighting posture called *tonbo gamae* (dragonfly stance) at a distance of five or six metres from the post. Following a long and loud exclamation of *kiai* (energy) he pounces upon the post at an appropriate distance and begins to strike it repeatedly.

The keynote of the Jigen-ryū was expressed in the phrase '*Asa ni sanzen, yu ni hassen*' ('three thousand in the morning and eight thousand in the evening') indicating the enormous repetition of the technique that was required. Striking a wooden post so many times was exhausting and painful to the limbs. Tōgō Shigekata had apparently first honed the technique by practising on living persimmon trees growing within the grounds of the Shimazu mansion until none were left!

87

Hayashi's Picture of a Catapult

石弾の図

While some samurai during the time of peace encouraged the practice of the martial arts among their colleagues others thought more widely and looked into Japan's strategic position within the isolation its policy had brought about.

The appearance of foreign ships off Japan's coast early in the nineteenth century concentrated many minds. It became obvious that Japan was not only lagging behind in military development, its exclusion from the outside world prevented any progress towards parity being made. A few bold scholars who served an equally small number of far-sighted daimyō did their best to learn from foreigners and apply the lessons to Japan's needs. Among them was Hayashi Shihei (1738-98), a scholar and retainer of the Sendai domain. Hayashi was an early advocate of the need for Japan to modernise its military capabilities against possible foreign aggression, a cause that was to become very popular as Japan's period of seclusion moved closer to its eventual end in 1854.

In 1791 Hayashi published *Kaikoku Heidan* ('Discourse on military matters for a maritime nation'), a work that drew on his own appetite for technology. As it was published without the consent of the Shogunate the printing blocks were confiscated soon afterwards, but when foreign ships began to be seen in Japanese waters the book was officially reprinted and grew steadily in importance. It consists of material drawn from overseas, particularly China, and includes several weird and wonderful machines. One is this exotic form of catapult, although the details of the catapult take various forms according to

the edition of the book one is examining. One version has the catapult mounted on a wheeled carriage. The type shown here (which is in the copy of Hayashi's book on display in Sendai City Museum in Japan) has the uprights sunk firmly into the ground.

A brief study of the catapult's mechanism indicates that it probably would work. The energy is provided by two large rocks joined by ropes, against which the firing arm is twisted, thus lifting the rocks to a higher position. The projectile would be placed in the net, and released using some form of trigger mechanism. Hayashi is clearly proud of this machine, because in the accompanying text he criticises those in authority who scorn the firearms and the other large weapons that he has described. Such devices, writes Hayashi, would be useful for coastal defence, a point completely lost on those who still believed that battles should consist of numerous noble individual sword combats. Personal comments like these probably helped towards getting the book banned, but is Hayashi describing something that really existed? The catapult machine does not appear ever to have been built and there are no other contemporary illustrations or descriptions of such a device, so the most likely conclusion is that Hayashi's drawing is an imaginative interpretation of something he has heard of during his researches. This

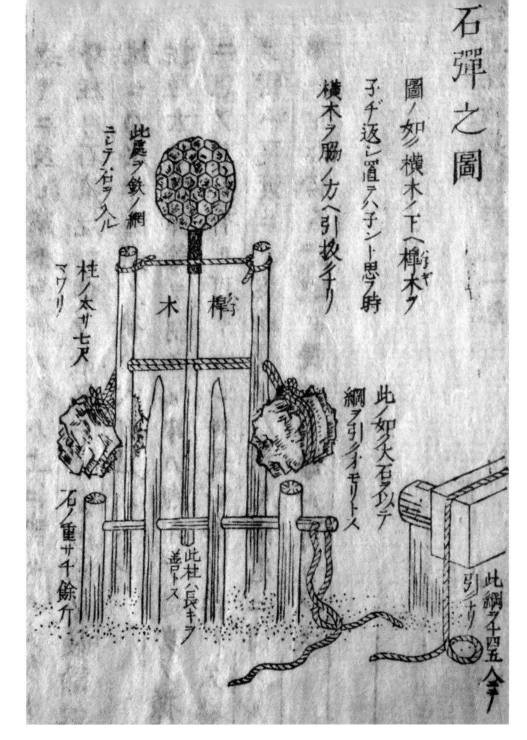

may have had a Chinese origin, and indeed the carriage bears a great similarity to contemporarily published Chinese illustrations of catapults, or it may even have come to Hayashi's attentions through the dissemination of *rangaku* (Dutch learning), that trickled through Japan's window on the outside world that was the Dutch trading post on Dejima in Nagasaki harbour. The source might therefore have been a reproduction of a European trebuchet, but the overwhelming element in the design was certainly Hayashi's vivid yet sincere imagination.

88

The Torture Rope of the Shinsengumi

新撰組の拷問縄

A man was once suspended from this rope and tortured, but the object has never been taken down and placed in a museum. Instead it still hangs limply from a roof beam in the storehouse of the former Maekawa residence in Kyōto, the actual site of the cruel interrogation by the Shinsengumi, 'the newly selected corps' who patrolled the capital. It led to the fiercest sword fight Kyōto had seen for many centuries and reminds us that the process whereby Japan became a modern nation was not just a peaceful one of building railways and steamships.

In 1854 an American fleet commanded by Commodore Matthew Perry had defied the two century-old ban on foreigners entering Japan and ended the country's self-imposed isolation. Trade negotiations followed, but the development was unwelcome to many in Japanese society. Whereas the supporters of the Shogun cooperated with the western nations by signing treaties and promoting trade, their opponents believed that the Shogun's acquiescence to western demands was a sign of weakness and a betrayal of traditional Japanese values. The rallying cry of these young activists was 'Revere the Emperor and Expel the Barbarians!'

This so-called 'loyalist' or 'imperialist' movement eventually came to believe that the main obstacle hindering the expulsion of the barbarians was the continued existence of the Shogun, who should be replaced by a restored imperial power. By 1864 the rival factions had spawned what were effectively terrorist organisations. So dangerous did the situation become that the Shogun appointed Matsudaira Katamori, the daimyō of Aizu, to protect

Kyōto against imperialist violence. Katamori recruited the swordsmen police who became known as the Shinsengumi.

Their first centre of operations was Mibu. Although it is now part of the city of Kyōto, Mibu still preserves a village atmosphere and the houses associated with the Shinsengumi are lovingly preserved. The Shinsengumi's headquarters were in the Maekawa residence from where their members patrolled the streets. Their most fanatical loyalist opponents were samurai from Chōshū at the far west of Honshū, and towards the end of May 1864 rumours were rife that Chōshū was planning to attack the imperial palace and kidnap the Emperor. The Shinsengumi learned that some Chōshū samurai had been meeting at the Ikedaya, an inn located close to the imperial palace. They already knew that a local shop-owner called Furutaka Shuntarō had sheltered loyalists, and a speculative raid on his shop revealed a cache of weapons. Shuntarō was taken back to the Maekawa house and hung upside down from this rope with his body dangling through a trapdoor. Long spikes were thrust

into his ankles and hot candle wax dripped was on to the wounds.

After half an hour of torture their prisoner revealed every detail of the plot. Ten of the Shisengumi's finest swordsmen then headed for the Ikedaya, where the Chōshū plotters appear to have mounted no guard. Instead they were upstairs getting drunk. The owner of the Ikedaya ran upstairs with the four Shinsengumi behind him. The desperate Chōshū samurai fought back like cornered rats. Seven were killed outright, with a further four dying later from their wounds while twenty-three of them were captured. Other sympathisers present with them were hunted down, some of them committing suicide in the streets round about to avoid the disgrace of capture. Elated by their victory, the Shinsengumi marched back to Mibu watched by crowds of onlookers, who gasped when the victorious samurai brandished their broken and damaged swords.

89

Statue of Katsura Kogorō of Chōshū

長州の桂 小五郎銅像

A defiant Katsura Kogorō (1834-1877) sits sword in hand with a knowing look upon his face. It proclaims to the citizens of modern Kyōto that in spite of the Shogun and his Shinsengumi it was the loyalist imperial cause that would eventually triumph and that Chōshū would be at the heart of the first government of modern Japan.

Also known as Kido Takayoshi, the name he later adopted, Kogorō was the chief negotiator on Chōshū's behalf with the other loyalist domains of Satsuma and Tosa in the discussions that eventually led to the three leading pro-imperial factions coming together. As an active loyalist living in Kyōto Kogorō was often a target of the Shinsengumi. He was supposed to attend the fatal meeting at the Ikedaya but received a tip off that the Shinsengumi were seeking him out. He therefore avoided the bloodbath of that night.

Chōshū's influence on the loyalist movement in Kyōto was greatly curtailed as a consequence of the Ikedaya massacre, but back in Chōshū itself the vehement loyalist resistance to foreigners took a very

different turn. Chōshū lay on the Straits of Shimonoseki between Honshu and Kyushu, a very important seaway for foreign vessels. In 1863 the daimyō of Chōshū ordered his gun batteries to fire without any warning on any foreign vessel passing through. So successful was the policy that the straits were effectively closed to foreign shipping until mid 1864.

Some token retaliatory gestures had been made, but not long after the Ikedaya Incident a massive international force sailed against their home territory. Within a day the Chōshū forts had been demolished and their troops defeated by foreign landing parties. The photograph shows this tremendous yet temporary humiliation for the loyalist cause.

An Imperial Activist from Tosa

土佐藩の志士

The rain lashes down on this bronze statue at Yusuhara on Shikoku Island, making it look as though its subject Nasu Shingo (1829-63) has sweat pouring off his forehead and tears in the eyes. He was one of the *shishi* (imperial activists) in the wars of the Meiji Restoration from the *han* (daimyō domain) of Tosa.

Following the accession of Tokugawa Yoshinobu in 1866 as the fifteenth and (as it turned out) final Shogun of Japan, the government had sought and obtained military assistance from foreign powers, and throughout the time of turmoil one asset that the Tokugawa possessed was that their loyalist opponents were divided among themselves.

Eventually the various factions united in a common cause. They were however still divided about how they should proceed towards their goal.

The moderate daimyō of Tosa, Yamanouchi Toyonori, proposed that Yoshinobu should resign as Shogun but continue to head a national council composed of daimyō. In order to bring this about Yoshinobu offered his resignation to the emperor on 9 November 1867 and formally stepped down ten days after that. He withdrew to Osaka Castle, but Satsuma and Chōshū were opposed to the compromise. For them the only way forward was the restoration of the emperor. This was now possible, so in January 1868 an alliance of Satsuma, Chōshū and other loyalist domains seized the Kyōto palace and

proclaimed the return of imperial rule in the person of Emperor Meiji.

As its first act, the new Meiji government stripped the Shogun of his lands and abolished all Shogunal offices. The ever-loyal Matsudaira Katamori was one among many to be taken by surprise by this dramatic operation. The Shogun Tokugawa Yoshinobu withdrew hurriedly to Osaka castle as Katamori marched at the head of 1,600 Aizu troops in an attempt to regain Kyōto. During the four days of the battle of Toba-Fushimi 120 Aizu samurai died and 158 were wounded.

The Shogun fled by ship to Edo. Matsudaira Katamori urged that eastern Japan should unite in a war against the traitors to the Shogun, but Tokugawa Yoshinobu was not for fighting. Instead he left Edo castle for a temple, where he waited to hear the decision of Japan's new rulers regarding his fate. Katamori retired to his domains in Aizu, protesting that he had shown no disloyalty to the emperor and had merely acted in self-defence against the act of aggression mounted by Satsuma and Chōshū. It was an aggression that was due to continue for some time.

Armour of the Satake Family

佐竹家の具足

The Shogun's abdication did not immediately mean the end of hostilities in the north of Japan. Many daimyō did not recognise the validity of his resignation and the Boshin War ('The War of the Year of the Dragon') began between the new imperial army of the restored Meiji Emperor and the supporters of the former Tokugawa Shogun.

Most of the fighting was confined to Tōhoku, where one of the imperial loyalists was Satake Yoshitaka (1825-84) the daimyō of Kubota (modern Akita City), and nothing better illustrates his ignorance of modern warfare than the equipment with which he sent his samurai off to fight. Unlike their rivals who had benefited from the good relationship between the Shogun and the Western powers to acquire modern guns and uniforms, the men of Akita were dressed in full samurai armour at least 300 years old complete with *jinbaori* (surcoats) and *sashimono* (flags) brought out from numerous family storerooms and possibly even museums. Their firearms were matchlock muskets and some even carried bows. At the battle of Toba-Fushimi a few months earlier Prince Yoshiaki had worn full samurai armour as a gesture to tradition when he commanded his modern army, but the Akita action was to be the last time in Japanese history that ordinary fighting troops were to be seen dressed this way.

Satake Yoshitaka (who never actually left the safety of his castle) ordered his army to stop the advance of the pro-Shogun Shōnai army in the narrow Misaki Pass, the border between modern Akita and Yamagata Prefectures, and it is interesting to find his army being led by men with the same surname as those who had served his ancestor Satake Yoshinobu at the siege of Osaka in 1614.

The overall command of the Akita army was in the hands of Shibue Naizen, who had an impeccable samurai pedigree. The Shibue family had been active in the encouragement and training of the Akita samurai in the traditional martial arts, but the amateurish attack that followed demonstrated dramatically how the domain had failed to keep up to date in military matters. The quaint appearance of the Akita army was paralleled by the expeditionary leader's equally amateurish and anachronistic behaviour. Little suspecting that the Shogun's army was waiting for him in the Misaki Pass, Arakawa Kūtarō confidently headed south with his army. As they passed through the village of Kisakata he stopped to do homage at the local Kumano Shrine, where he cut off his pigtail like a samurai general of old and presented it to the shrine as an offering for victory.

When the forces engaged the brilliantly lacquered breastplates and helmets bearing the golden *mon* of the Satake family shone in the sunlight of dawn, making them the perfect target for the waiting rifles of the Shogun's force. There was so much confusion that the Akita men began attacking each other by mistake, and this disastrous first attempt at warfare on the part of the Akita domain for two and a half centuries came to an abrupt end.

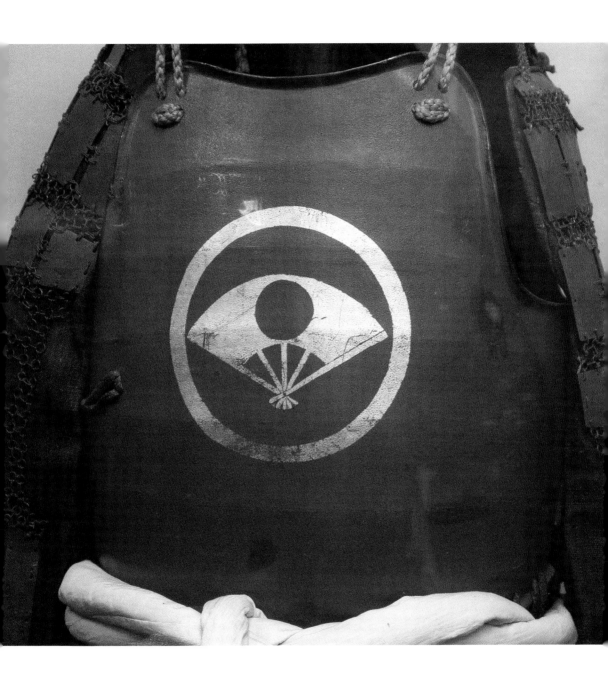

92

Photograph of Ikoma Chikayuki

生駒近行の写真

Two weeks after forcing the Misaki Pass, the Shogun's army advanced on the domain of Yashima. Yashima lay under the control of 19-year-old Ikoma Chikayuki (1849-80), who was destined to become the first daimyō in the Akita area to face a hostile attack in his own territory for 250 years.

During the peaceful Edo Period most daimyō had maintained the samurai tradition only as a theoretical concept, having lost not only the ability to fight but even the notion that being a samurai had something to do with waging war. Progressive daimyō closer to the centre of power such as Shōnai and Chōshū had already dealt with the situation and were now leading the rival sides in the Boshin War, but certain daimyō in the remote area of Tōhoku, to whom the word samurai meant 'aristocrat' rather than 'warrior', were soon to have a very rude awakening. This photograph shows one of them.

When the Boshin War began tiny Yashima was a place where any daimyō might feel secure because the only practical access to the isolated fiefdom was from Honjō in the north. Nowadays a branch line from Honjō takes skiers up to the mountain resort that Yashima has become, where it nestles beneath the mighty bulk of Mount Chōkai (2,236 metres), the second highest mountain in Tōhoku. So secure was Ikoma Chikayuki's domain that his ancestors had not built a castle but instead ruled from a modest unfortified mansion.

The Shōnai army advanced against him during the month of September, which provided a brief window of opportunity for a daring assault over the summit of Mount Chōkai. On 13 September 1868 the mountain's southern face was scaled by the Shōnai IV Corps. The army spent the night in the Ōmonoimi Shrine just below the summit (shown in the smaller picture) and as dawn broke they descended by rough paths of scree and old snow down the northern side. Ikoma Chikayuki was taken completely by surprise and fled to the north as temples, houses and his own precious mansion burned around him.

A few days later a second young daimyō was to experience an attack by the Shōnai army. This was Rokugō Masaakira (1848-1907), then twenty years old, who ruled the domain of Honjō. Like Ikoma, Rokugō was the descendant of warriors, but samurai ancestry was all that the young Masaakira possessed in abundance, so he prepared as

best he could for an assault. However, in accordance with the overall strategy from imperial headquarters, he was told that Honjō was to be abandoned and that his army had to withdraw to Akita. When Masaakira left Honjō he was horrified to see his magnificent castle being burned down by the retreating imperial forces so that it would not fall into the hands of their enemies. In these painful ways two nominal leaders of samurai had become warriors once again.

93

A Boshin War Graveyard

戊辰戦争墓地

This dramatic standing stone marks the entrance to the graveyard of the Ryōshō-In at Yokote (Akita Prefecture) which provides the resting place for some of the bravest fighters in the Boshin War, because while one army from Shōnai was destroying Yashima and Honjō another was heading inland towards Yokote Castle.

In 1615 Satake Yoshinobu had installed as its keeper the grandson of Tomura Yoshikuni, whose bravery was noted earlier and whose effigy still stands in the Ryōshō-In. Responsibility for Yokote stayed within the Tomura family over the next two centuries, and when the Shōnai army advanced on Yokote in 1868 a 19-year-old descendant of Yoshikuni called Tomura Daigaku was waiting for them. Like Rokugō Masaakira of Honjō, Daigaku was ordered to retreat, but the proud commander of Yokote castle refused to obey orders because he was the retainer of a daimyō to whom he had pledged loyalty and who had solemnly entrusted him with the defence of the castle. The Tomura had been the keepers of Yokote since the time of his ancestors, and to abandon that solemn responsibility would be to dishonour their spirits. How could he ever show his face in the presence of his lord again? Instead he stated, 'I shall fight until my strength runs out, and then die in action with the castle as my pillow.' With a garrison of only 280 men, Tomura Daigaku decided to withstand the entire Shōnai army of 3,000 men on his own.

No greater example of stubborn yet ultimately doomed samurai heroism was to be displayed in the whole of the Boshin War as Tomura Daigaku demonstrated that he was the equal of his illustrious ancestor Tomura Yoshikuni, whose glaring glass eyes still stared down on his descendants. Yet even though Daigaku's samurai spirit was still alive he had little in the way of food supplies. His armaments also demonstrated the overall imperialist strategy of not wasting modern weapons in the defence of an expendable position.

Of hand-held firearms there were two modern rifles and thirty-eight old matchlock muskets. Besides these he had bows and spears. Apart from that he had bravery, determination, and a great respect for the traditions of his ancestors. The climax of the battle came on 26 September with two hours of fierce hand-to-hand fighting during which Tomura Daigaku killed two men with his own sword. Seeing that the cause was now hopeless he prepared himself for the act of *seppuku*. He was urged against it by one of his officers and instead led a fighting retreat out of the castle. Daigaku's own story does in fact have a happy ending, because he somehow survived the Boshin War and went on to become the Mayor of Yokote. An oil painting of him hangs in the Ryōshō-In next to the funerary chapel of Tomura Yoshikuni. With ancestors like that you don't surrender!

The Statues of the Ōmura Drummer Boy

大村藩少年鼓手銅像

The final battle of the Boshin War was fought at Kariwano in Akita Prefecture, and its saddest victim is commemorated by two identical statues erected over 2,000km apart.

They represent a drummer boy aged fifteen, whose death was to become a symbolic one. His name was Hamada Kingyō and he became one of the last soldiers to die during the campaign. He was almost certainly the youngest, because Japanese armies, copying European ones, had introduced drummer boys into their forces. When he died a letter from his parents was found on his body that included a poem written by his mother urging him to be brave. He is remembered in two places: at Kakunodate in Akita and back in his home town of Ōmura in Nagasaki Prefecture where the same statue stands. Even more moving than the statues however, is the direction sign next to the one at Kakunodate that states that the youth died 2,240 kilometres from home.

Sadly, the battle of Kariwano was one that should have been avoided. The retreating imperialists had made a final stand at Tsubakidai Castle, which Satake Yoshitaka ordered to be held at all costs. The Shōnai army faced them from high ground across the river to the south. The fighting was intense, but the imperialist line held. The following day the imperialists went on to the attack supported by cannon fire from forward positions and drove the Shōnai army back, inflicting casualties on them of 100 dead and eighty wounded, the greatest

single loss by the Shōnai army since the campaign had begun. Thirty percent of the houses in the area were burned down and many local villagers lost their lives.

The decisive battle of Tsubakidai was the turning point in the Akita-Shōnai Campaign, but one section of the Shōnai army had retreated along the old road north of the river towards the river crossing at Kakunodate. Unable to complete their journey they made a last-ditch stand at Kariwano. At dawn on 31 October, with their bullets almost used up and their bodies exhausted, the Shōnai army finished their long campaign against Akita in a consummate illustration of the samurai tradition by making a final desperate charge with their samurai swords. Both sides were now exhausted, but because of Tsubakidai the slaughter at Kariwano was meaningless, and among the dead lay a little drummer boy.

A Bullet Hole

弾痕

Six bullet holes from modern rifles still remain in the walls and doors of the Takigawa Honjin, the building that provided the field headquarters for the Shogun's army at Aizu. They remind us that the Boshin War saw heroics and poignant moments on both sides of the conflict.

In Akita the imperialists are the heroes. In Aizu-Wakamatsu in modern Fukushima Prefecture the troops loyal to the Shogun are remembered, both for the fierce last-ditch stand they put up against the Imperial Army and for the severe treatment that was then meted out to them. One of the most vivid memorials of the fighting is this battered building.

The main objective of the Imperial Army advance was Aizu's Tsugaru Castle. Their troops burned the samurai houses in the outer castle precincts while fifty cannon pounded the castle day and night. On 6 November 1868, one month after the siege had begun, a white flag was raised above the northern gate. During the nine months between the battle of Toba-Fushimi that had seen the Shogun driven out of Kyōto and the fall of Aizu-Wakamatsu castle, 2,610 Aizu men had died in action. Great bravery was shown by all ages and from all social classes in the defence of the domain. As far as Aizu was concerned they represented the legitimate government of the Shogun but were no less loyal to the sacred person of the Emperor because of it. The Meiji rulers who defeated them took a different view, so in a cruel act of retribution the entire domain was confiscated and the surviving samurai were sent to detention camps.

Some time around the beginning of 1870 the infant son of the former daimyō Matsudaira Katamori was given permission to revive the family name and line, but he was not restored to Aizu. Instead he was granted lands on the Shimokita Peninsula in what is now Aomori Prefecture.

It was a barren land of volcanic ash buried for half the year in snow. The samurai detainees were allowed to leave their camps for their new homeland in the spring of 1870. They were not up to farming the inhospitable land and many perished from malnutrition and disease. Local villagers who saw them eating wild plants and roots called them the 'Aizu caterpillars'. The punishment inflicted upon Aizu surpassed in vindictiveness the treatment of any other rebels during the wars of the Meiji Restoration. No other opponents of the new order in Japan saw seen their lands confiscated, their samurai sent into detention and their people exiled.

96

Oka Castle in Ōita prefecture

岡城

How beautiful it must once have looked, proclaims this painting on silk of Oka Castle, and how melancholy now are its massive stone bases and walls, overgrown by vegetation! Its ruins still sprawl along a wooded and mountainous ridge overlooking the town of Bungo-Takada in Ōita prefecture on the island of Kyushu to make one of Japan's most impressive ruined castle sites.

Mount Gagyu on which it lies was first fortified in 1185 by the family of Ogata, who were sympathetic to the Minamoto family at the time of the Gempei War. Although associated romantically with the name of Minamoto Yoshitsune, its history properly begins with Shiga Sadatomo in 1332. The Shiga family ruled Oka until 1586, by which time they had become close allies of the Ōtomo and accepted Christian baptism. Shiga Tarō Chikatsugu took the name of Paul, and unlike many of his neighbours stood firm when the Shimazu clan invaded their territory. Oka castle proved to be ideal as a base from where guerrilla attacks could be mounted against the Shimazu.

In the redistribution of territory which followed Hideyoshi's conquest of Kyushu Oka castle was given to Nakagawa Hidenari (1570-1612). He was responsible for rebuilding the edifice in the form it was to retain, and the experienced Katō Kiyomasa assisted in the planning of Oka's layout. In 1663 the castle was greatly expanded by the construction of the Nishi-no-maru (Western Bailey).

The keep was destroyed by an earthquake during the Edo Period, while the remaining superstructure was demolished during the Meiji Period as one of many similar examples whereby local communities demonstrated their abandonment of the feudal past and their association with the new Japan. Demolition indicated loyalty to the Meiji Emperor and also showed that Japan was modern and forward-looking. Ironically, the beautiful castles like Himeji and Hirosaki that survive to this day were not preserved out of love; their owners were too poor to afford the cost of demolishing them! Oka was thoroughly destroyed down to its unshakeable bases.

Having been abandoned in 1871, Oka Castle was designated a national historic site in 1936, and has today been attractively landscaped. Weeds now cover the walls on which the elaborate superstructure of a magnificent castle once sat.

去こ梅ここ九の宴
をくる盃野をこ亭
千代の栢か枝もふゆよし
むや〳〵の光にいづき

秋神々蛍の露の色
時る見く雁の虹みゆへ
椎るつきに惜みのひ
昔のひ乱り〳〵にいてこ

て荒珠の杜まれ月
嘉合光るかためか
垣ほ越る峰かつう
松に歌ゆ日たゝ嵐

天上野れ裏らねて
繁栢日稲今世の姿
寫光とうれら四片
方。荒塚の松まつ月

晩年

97

An Armour of
mogami haramaki Style

最上腹巻

Many suits of Japanese armour have been illustrated in this book, but none has travelled more widely than this interesting piece..

A description of it from a London sale catalogue of 1841 missed the mark completely when it listed it as typical of those 'worn by the Moors of Granada prior to their expulsion from Spain', a phrase that, if nothing else, shows how effective Japan's seclusion policy was when it came to the dissemination of information to nineteenth-century Britain. The armour is in fact undoubtedly Japanese and is a curious blend of two popular armour styles. A *mogami-dō* is a body armour made from five separate hinged sections that fit neatly together round the torso. A *haramaki*, typically constructed in the old lamellar style, is literally a 'body-wrapper' that opens only at the back along the length of the spine.

Just like the armour presented to King James I this object was probably a diplomatic gift. As it ended up in the Spanish Royal Armoury one may presume that it was a present for the King of Spain, but it is by no means clear when it was presented to his envoys. It may have been one of the gifts sent to Europe along with the embassy provided by four Christian Japanese youths in 1582. That extraordinary mission was sponsored by the Christian daimyō Ōtomo Sōrin, and their eight-year-long tour included audiences with two successive Popes and meetings with King Philip II of Spain among others. It is known that the gifts for the king included two suits of Japanese armour. The armour eventually made its way via the Spanish Royal Armoury to the sale in London in 1841, where it was bought by the Tower of London.

Even more tantalising than its European tour are the little details on the armour that provide possible clues to its status and ownership prior to being given to Philip II. The most fascinating speculation is provided by the *mon*, which is of a cross within a circle. The *mon* could be a variation on the 'cross within a ring' *mon* of the Shimazu of Satsuma. That usually took a heavily stylised geometric form derived from the end of a horse's bit, but a more elongated cross was also known.

However, the cross also looks very much like a Christian cross, and it was once suggested that the armour belonged to Naitō Yukiyasu, a Christian daimyō who was exiled to Manila. Its provenance as a diplomatic gift is much more likely, and if it accompanied the embassy of the Christian youths such a bold symbol of their faith would not have been out of place.

98

'Cherry blossom' Suicide Plane

桜花特攻兵器

It is called an 'Ōka' (cherry blossom), but the object itself is very different in nature from the fragile flowers that surround the statue at Ōgaki. This cherry blossom is cold and clinical, a manned flying bomb made for death alone.

It hangs from the ceiling of the Yūshūkan, the military museum of the Yasukuni Shrine in Tokyo. Slung beneath the belly of a bomber it was carried within range of its target and released. The pilot would first fly it as a glider, and when he came within sight of his target he would fire the Ōka's rocket engine and dive towards the ship he intended to destroy. Most of the 750 Ōka aircraft built were never launched, having been shot down while still attached to their carrying aircraft. Of the ones that were released it is thought that about fifteen Allied ships were sunk by their impact.

Japan's suicide weapons were given a heroic cultural tinge that derived from the samurai tradition. The choice of a cherry blossom for the manned flying bomb is an obvious allusion to a dying warrior and has echoes of the ancient association noted earlier. A different link is made in the smaller picture. It is a manned suicide torpedo, the underwater equivalent of the

Ōka. Painted on to its side is the chrysanthemum on the water *mon* of Kusunoki Masashige, the emperor's most loyal samurai. As for the name by which these suicide weapons and their attacks were usually known - 'kamikaze' – that name derived from the 'wind from the gods' that

The naval units who carried them out were known as shinpū *tokubetsu kōgeki tai* (divine wind attack units), *shinpū* being the Chinese-style reading of the two-character compound otherwise read as *kamikaze*. That word was common among the Allied troops and was reimported into Japan after the war. In such ways did old words associated with samurai acquire terrifying new meanings.

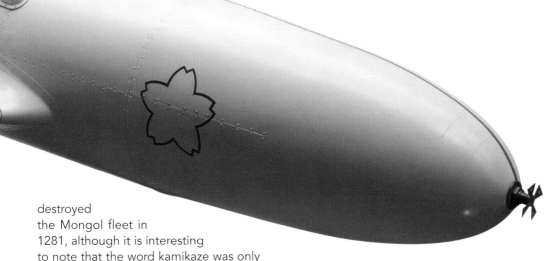

destroyed
the Mongol fleet in
1281, although it is interesting
to note that the word kamikaze was only
used casually in Japan to refer to the units
known officially as the *tokubetsu kōgeki tai*
(special attack units).

197

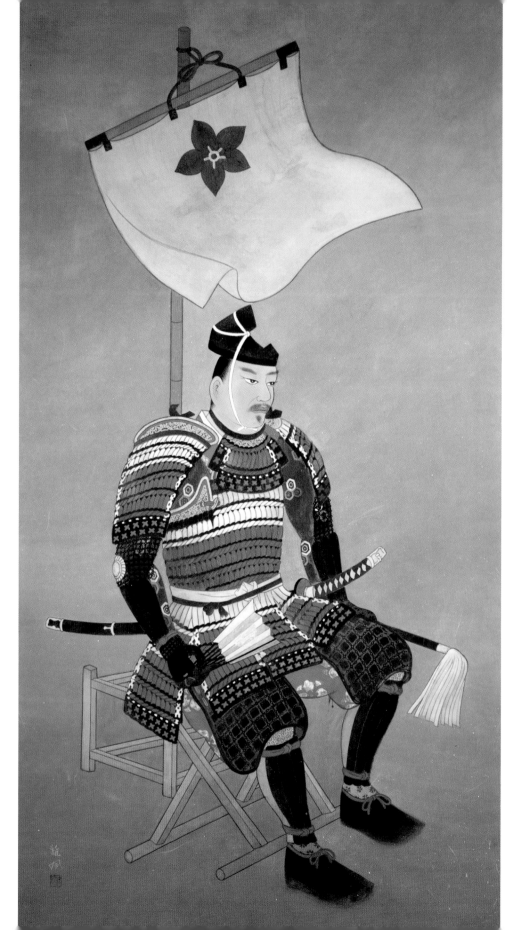

Akechi Mitsuhide and Fukuchiyama Castle

明智光秀と福知山城

As Japan's cities began to rebuild and recover after the devastation of the Second World War, so too did the samurai tradition begin to re-invent itself, and these pictures illustrate how the processes of rehabilitation took place.

world long gone. The 1950s and 1960s then saw a revival of interest and a reawakening of pride. All round the country Japanese castles that had once been patriotically demolished by their citizens were enthusiastically rebuilt with varying results in terms of quality or accuracy. Fukuchiyama is one the best examples. It has a concrete core but wood has been used very effectively.

The painting is of Akechi Mitsuhide, celebrated in his former castle town but reviled everywhere else as the worst traitor in Japanese history. He was the general who took Oda Nobunaga by surprise at the Honnōji temple in 1582.

A few days later he received a rapid revenge attack from Toyotomi Hideyoshi. Mitsuhide fled from the battlefield and was beaten to death by a gang of peasants. His image as a turncoat is therefore similar to that of Ashikaga Takauji, but this modern painting depicts him romantically as the ideal samurai. It hangs inside his rebuilt castle of Fukuchiyama where he is greatly celebrated.

The new Fukuchiyama Castle is the product of another form of rehabilitation. Post-1945 Japan had to deal with a backlash against militarism so the samurai were pushed back into history, inspiring maybe, but images of a

Restored or rebuilt Japanese castles can now be found all over the country, and the strangest rebuild of all is Kameda Castle in Akita Prefecture. In 1868 its young lord Iwaki Takakuni saw what was happening to his neighbours at Yashima and Honjō so he immediately changed sides in order to save his home from destruction, but a fierce battle drove the Shōnai troops back and the imperialists won. The Akita forces then took terrible revenge on the treacherous Iwaki by burning Kameda Castle to the ground.

In the boom years of 1960s Japan the decision was taken to rebuild the castle. But where should it be built, at the place it originally occupied or somewhere more convenient for visitors? A compromise was reached, and Kameda was rebuilt twice, so you can now visit Kameda Castle and then drive a short distance to see another Kameda Castle!

A Cute Samurai

かわいい侍

Kawaii is the quality of cuteness within modern Japanese culture. Something that is kawaii is sweet, loveable and adorable, and how cute is this little blue duck on sale in the souvenir shop at Kumamoto Station?

He is dressed as a samurai complete with helmet, spear and surcoat, but he is not just any samurai, he represents Kumamoto's greatest ever daimyō Katō Kiyomasa, whom we have encountered before. He owned a 'strange helmet' (copied here on the duck). He led the merciless attack on the castle of Hondo in 1589 and then almost came to blows with Konishi Yukinaga during the invasion of Korea where he would experience the bitter siege of Ulsan Castle.

That Katō Kiyomasa could become a child's toy is remarkable considering the life its subject had led, and Katō Kiyomasa's personal journey from daimyō to duck is probably the most extreme result of the modern processes of change and reinterpretation discussed above for Akechi Mitsuhide. An early companion of Toyotomi Hideyoshi, Kiyomasa fought at the battle of Shizugatake in 1583. His rise to fame came with his transfer to Higo Province and his suppression of the Amakusa rebels in 1589-90, where his ruthlessness was contrasted earlier with the act of mercy to the defenders shown by Konishi Yukinaga. In addition to leading a rampaging army through the Korean peninsula he is believed to have committed several personal acts of atrocity including the murder of a girl captive. After the Korean War he developed Kumamoto as a fine castle town, where he was greatly honoured and respected. Now he is also *kawaii*.

The Katō Kiyomasa duck is not Kumamoto City's official mascot. That honour is reserved for a rather fine *kawaii* bear called Kumamon, but in Hikone (Shiga Prefecture) its former daimyō lives on as Hikonyan, a sweet white pussy cat wearing a helmet. Hikonyan (the name derives from 'Hikone miaow') was created in 2010 and is based on a legend linking Ii Naomasa to a white cat that invited him to seek shelter inside a temple during a storm. It saved him from being struck by lightning.

Hikonyan is now one of the most popular city mascots in Japan. In the smaller picture a guide dressed as Hikonyan welcomes visitors to Hikone Castle in 2015. He wears the Ii red armour with golden horns that once shone above the bloody battlefield of Sekigahara. This *kawaii* mascot exemplifies the greatest historical transition that the samurai ever made: a long journey from fearless warriors to cuddly toys.

Picture Credits and Locations

1. Gate of Akita Castle: Akita City.
    Diorama of an official: Tagajō Castle Site Museum, Tagajō, Miyagi Prefecture.
2. Netsuke of two samurai: Private Collection.
3. Quiver: Ann and Gabriel Barbier-Mueller Collection.
4. Samurai Helmet: Royal Armouries Museum, Leeds.
5. Gosannen War Scroll: Gosannen War Museum, Gosannen, Akita Prefecture.
6. Tachi: Royal Armouries Museum, Leeds.
7. Niō: Miyajima, Hiroshima Prefecture.
    Nagamaki: Royal Armouries Museum, Leeds.
8. Head viewing Print: Private Collection.
9. Itsukushima Shrine, Miyajima, Hiroshima Prefecture.
    Print: Private Collection.
10. Yoshitsune's helmet: Kuramadera, Kyoto.
11. Tomoe Gozen Print: Courtesy of Lella and Gianni Morra, Fine Japanese Prints, Illustrated Books and Works of Art, Venice, Italy.
12. Heike Crab: Author's Collection.
    Tomomori Print: Author's Collection.
13. Mongol Bomb: Kyushu National Museum.
    Scroll: Private Collection.
14. Chrysanthemum Design: Yoshino, Nara Prefecture.
    Painting: Nyoirinji, Yoshino.
15. Temple Door and Painting: Nyoirinji, Yoshino.
16. Ashikaga Takauji Statue: Tōji-In, Kyoto.
17. Boki Ekotoba: Nishi-Honganji, Kyoto.
18. Wakizashi: Royal Armouries Museum, Leeds.
19. Wakō Painting: National Military Museum, Beijing.
20. Kinkakuji: Kinkakuji, Kyoto.
21. Marishiten Scroll: Nakajima Collection.
22. Helmet with Fudō: Ann and Gabriel Barbier-Mueller Collection.
23. Katana: Royal Armouries Museum, Leeds.
24. Openwork Tower: Arata Castle, Ueda, Nagano Prefecture.
25. Scroll with spear fighting: Ueda Castle, Ueda, Nagano Prefecture.
26. Arquebus: Ann and Gabriel Barbier-Mueller Collection.
27. Uesugi Kenshin Scroll: Private Collection.
28. Kosaka Scroll: Erinji Museum, Enzan, Yamanashi Prefecture.
    Ema: Author's Collection.
29. Matsu Hime statue and naginata: Shinsho-In, Hachiōji, Tokyo.

30. Itagaki Scroll: Erinji Museum, Enzan,Yamanashi Prefecture.
31. Okegawa-dō: Sekigahara Museum, Sekigahara, Gifu Prefecture.
32. Anegawa Screen: Fukui Prefectural Museum.
33. War Drum: Mitsuke School Museum, Iwata, Shizuoka Prefecture.
    Sakai Print: Author's Collection.
34. Torii Sune'emon: Nagashino Castle Preservation Hall, Nagashino, Aichi Prefecture.
    Screen: Nakatsu Castle, Nakatsu, Fukuoka Prefecture.
35. Gohei Standard: Ueda Castle, Nagano Prefecture.
    Menju Print: Author's Collection.
36. Stone Head and Shibata statue: Saikoji, Fukui City.
37. Portuguese cannon and gun emplacement: Usuki Castle, Usuki, Ōita Prefecture.
38. Tanaka map: Yamaguchi Prefectural Library.
39. Kai Shrine: Kashima, Kumamoto City.
    Yufu grave: Nagomi, Kumamoto Prefecture.
40. Gōganji, Nakatsu, Fukuoka Prefecture.
41. Bernardo Nagasaki Statue: Nagasaki Park, Nagasaki City.
42. Kato Yoshiaki Print: Author's Collection.
43. Konishi Yukinaga Print: Author's Collection.
44. Haengju Castle and Statue: Haengju, Seoul, South Korea.
45. Mōri Armour: Ann and Gabriel Barbier-Mueller Collection.
    Statue: Mihara Station, Hiroshima Prefecture.
46. Elephant Statue: Ayutthaya, Thailand.
47. Matsumoto Castle: Matsumoto, Nagano Prefecture.
48. Screen of Ulsan: Nagoya Castle Museum, Karatsu, Saga Prefecture.
    Print: Author's Collection.
49. Fujito Rock: Sanbo-In, Daigōji, Kyoto.
50. Bloody Ceiling: Hōsen-In, Ōhara, Kyōto.
51. Sekigahara Screen: Sekigaharaland, Sekigahara, Gifu Prefecture.
    Battlefield at Sekigahara.
52. Ii Armour: Royal Armouries Museum, Leeds.
53. Tachibana Armour: Tachibana Museum, Ohana, Yanagawa, Fukuoka Prefecture.
54. Arima Statue: Daiunji, Maruoka, Fukui Prefecture.
55. Toda Statue: Ōgaki Castle, Ōgaki, Gifu Prefecture.
    Cherry blossom: Kakunodate, Akita Prefecture.
56. Book Illustrations: Nara Prefectural Library.
57. Nakijin and Katsuren Gusuku: Okinawa Prefecture.
58. Maeda Helmet: Toyama Castle Museum, Toyama Prefecture.
    Statue: Kanazawa Castle, Kanazawa City, Ishikawa Prefecture.
59. Namban Helmets: Ohana, Yanagawa, Fukuoka Prefecture.
60. Uto Tower: Kumamoto Castle, Kumamoto City.
61. Shakujō Standard and Statue: Hirosaki Castle, Hirosaki, Aomori Prefecture.
62. Miyamoto Musashi Painting: Shimada Art Museum, Kumamoto City.

63. Armour of King James I : Royal Armouries Museum, Leeds.
64. Temple Bell: Hōkōji, Kyoto.
65. Tomura Statue: Ryōshō-In, Yokote, Akita Prefecture.
66. Sanada ema: Author's Collection.
67. Hachisuka Painting: Tokushima Castle Museum.
    Jingasa: Hirosaki Castle, Hirosaki, Aomori Prefecture.
68. Daimyō Armour: Royal Armouries Museum, Leeds.
    Jinbaori: Kakunodate, Akita Prefecture.
69. Shōki Banner: Kakunodate, Akita Prefecture.
    Shōkisama: Taga Shrine, Ōmaki, Niigata Prefecture.
70. Yukinoshita-dō: Royal Armouries Museum, Leeds.
    Date Statue: Sendai Castle, Sendai City.
71. Ema of Yamada Nagamasa: Nihonmachi, Ayutthaya, Thailand.
    Ruins: Ayutthaya.
72. Christian Tea Bowl: Shimabara Castle Museum, Shimabara City, Nagasaki Prefecture.
73. Shigemasa's Grave: Shimabara, Nagasaki Prefecture.
    Skull: Hara Castle Museum, Nagasaki Prefecture.
74. Helmet with hare's ears: Royal Armouries Museum, Leeds.
75. Swimming Scroll: Nakajima Collection.
    Photograph: Kumamoto Castle.
76. Ear Mound and Painting.
    Matsumae Castle, Matsumae, Hokkaidō.
77. Mansenshūkai: Kōka Ninja House, Kōka, Shiga Prefecture.
    Ninja: Toei Studio Park, Kyoto.
78. Matsuura Scroll: Matsuura Historical Museum, Hirado, Nagasaki Prefecture.
79. Fan: Ōishi Shrine, Banshū-Ako, Okayama Prefecture.
    Statue: Outside Banshū-Ako Station.
80. Fire cloak and helmet: Ann and Gabriel Barbier-Mueller Collection.
81. Tsuba: Maruoka Castle, Maruoka City, Fukui Prefecture.
82. Conch Shell Trumpet: University Museum, Manchester, UK.
83. Antler Helmet: Fukuchiyama Castle, Fukuchiyama, Kyoto Prefecture.
    Statue: Kuwana Castle site, Kuwana, Mie Prefecture.
84. Human Head Helmet: Ann and Gabriel Barbier-Mueller Collection.
    Facemask: Matsue Castle, Matsue, Shimane Prefecture.
85. Horse Armour: Ann and Gabriel Barbier-Mueller Collection.
86. Training Pole and Scroll: Jigen-ryū Dōjō, Kagoshima City.
87. Catapult illustration: Sendai City Museum, Miyagi Prefecture.
88. Torture rope: Maekawa House, Mibu, Kyoto.
89. Statue of Kogorō: near Kyoto City Hall.
    Photograph: Chōshū Battery Monument, Shimonoseki, Yamaguchi Prefecture.
90. Statue: Yusuhara, Kōchi Prefecture.
91. Satake Breastplate: Kakunodate, Akita Prefecture.

92. Ikoma Photograph: Akita Prefectural Museum.
    Shrine: Mount Chōkai, Akita Prefecture.
93. Gravestone: Ryōshō-In, Yokote City, Akita Prefecture.
94. Drummer Boy Statue and Sign: Kakunodate, Akita Prefecture.
95. Bullet Hole: Takigawa Honjin, Aizu-Wakamatsu, Fukushima Prefecture.
96. Oka Castle Scroll and Ruins: Oka Castle Site, Bungo-Takada, Ōita Prefecture.
97. Armour: Royal Armouries Museum, Leeds.
98. Kamikaze Plane: Yūshūkan, Yasukuni Shrine, Tokyo.
99. Akechi Scroll and Fukuchiyama Castle: Fukuchiyama, Kyoto Prefecture.
100. Katō Kiyomasa figure: Author's Collection.
    Hikonyan: Hikone Castle, Hikone City, Shiga Prefecture.